BUSINESS
DOING GOOD

BUSINESS DOING GOOD

Engaging Women and Elevating Communities

**Shannon Deer and
Cheryl Miller**

ROWMAN & LITTLEFIELD
Lanham • Boulder • New York • London

Published by Rowman & Littlefield
An imprint of The Rowman & Littlefield Publishing Group, Inc.
4501 Forbes Boulevard, Suite 200, Lanham, Maryland 20706
www.rowman.com

6 Tinworth Street, London SE11 5AL, United Kingdom

British Library Cataloguing in Publication Information Available

Library of Congress Cataloging-in-Publication Data

Names: Deer, Shannon, 1981– author. | Miller, Cheryl, 1958– author.
Title: Business doing good : engaging women and elevating communities /
  Shannon Deer and Cheryl Miller.
Description: Lanham : Rowman & Littlefield Publishers, 2021. | Includes
  bibliographical references and index.
Identifiers: LCCN 2020056329 (print) | LCCN 2020056330 (ebook) | ISBN
  9781538152379 (cloth) | ISBN 9781538152386 (epub)
Subjects: LCSH: Women—Employment. | Homeless women—Employment.
  | Poor women—Employment. | Skilled labor—Training of. | Equality before
  the law. | Sex discrimination against women. | Diversity in the workplace.
Classification: LCC HD6053 .D44 2021 (print) | LCC HD6053 (ebook) |
  DDC 658.3/1108694—dc23
LC record available at https://lccn.loc.gov/2020056329
LC ebook record available at https://lccn.loc.gov/2020056330

CONTENTS

INTRODUCTION

Two or three things I know for sure, and one of them is that to go on living I have to tell stories, that stories are the one sure way I know to touch the heart and change the world.

—Dorothy Allison

In 2004, Unilever's Dove brand, along with its public relations firm, released its Real Beauty ads campaign that changed the way women thought about beauty. Dove backed up the campaign with initiatives to improve women's self-esteem, which it continues today. These initiatives included the development of curriculum to help parents raise confident children and for schools and youth leaders to teach body confidence. It also launched #GirlCollective, which includes a conference and groups to support girls. Its self-esteem education now reaches more than twenty million young people.[1] The Real Beauty campaign for Dove was a natural extension of the company's commitment to contributing to social good and almost doubled sales.

Unilever already had a platform for business practices designed for a greater good, as a leader in successful corporate social responsibility (CSR) initiatives. CSR "encompasses responsible or sustainable business practices with a focus on people, planet, and profit."[2] CSR, or a focus on environmental, social, and governance (ESG) issues, has become more widely adopted by CEOs because investors and consumers demand more than just profit from companies.

What do Unilever, Johnson & Johnson, Google, and Lego have in common? Sure, they are giant companies with huge profits, but they are also companies that have done good for the world through commitments to CSR that have permeated their culture.

For example, Johnson & Johnson's 2018 sustainability report, Health for Humanity Report, noted that it now obtains 31 percent of its electricity sources from renewable energy. It also educated more than 104,000 health workers in sixty-seven countries. Such initiatives positively impact the company's bottom line—profit—by reducing costs through renewables and increasing affinity for its products through health education. Further, it makes a positive impact on the other components of the triple bottom line—planet, through renewables, and people, through health education.[3]

Similarly, Google operates carbon neutral, is committed to renewable energy,[4] and has touted its positive workplace reputation for employee rewards, well-being, and equal opportunities.[5] Lego released plant-based products as an alternative to plastic in 2018 to improve its environmental impact but also to attract millennial consumers demanding sustainable toys, thus benefitting both the consumer and its bottom line.[6]

In business today, competition is steeper, and innovation is faster than it has ever been. And as business leaders, we are responsible for addressing some significant challenges, including:

- Gaps in human capital (i.e., a shortage of qualified employees),
- A need for increased diversity in teams,
- Pressure for companies to move beyond profit-only motives to people and planet consciousness,
- Awakening to sexual harassment in the workplace, with little training to address it,
- Expectations to adopt emerging technologies, and
- Increased regulation.

The challenges companies face today and the problems they are expected to tackle are bigger than those of the past. It's the nature of progress: We have solved the easy problems, and what is left are more challenging. Further, there is increased pressure from investors and society to be better and to have a more positive impact on society, while maintaining costs.

A friend described his professional life as having two peaks. The first peak represented the success he had already had in business. He was now excited to be on the second peak, where he could focus on giving back to others. The philosophy is similar to that popularized in David Brooks's *The Second Mountain*, shifting from an individualized focus to a life committed to meaning and purpose.[7] Wherever you are in your journey—any peak or valley—we hope to meet you there with this book. If you are reading this, we imagine you desire to make an impact on the world. You may have recently finished school and are looking up to the peak of the first mountain. This book could provide you a unique way to make an impact in your organization early and differentiate yourself. If you are summiting the first peak in your career now, having built a successful business or reached a high-level position, then the principles in this book can help you take your organization to the next level using the influence you have earned. Perhaps, you are looking for an opportunity to define your second peak.

Anywhere along the journey, we hope by reading this book that you will be motivated to address the big challenges facing business and society today. If your business is trying to make a difference with effective corporate responsibility, you will find ideas and tools proven to increase your ability to impact society and also grow profitability. You will discover innovative concepts that will allow people the greatest opportunity to live their dreams and discover the incredible potential within. We hope you also find encouragement and recognize your own experiences in the voices of those found on these pages. Our biggest desire is that you will find what you need to persevere and journey on farther and deeper than you ever realized.

WHY INVEST IN WOMEN?

Although there are many ways businesses can make an impact, we make a case that investing in women can be the most significant. Investing in women advances families, communities, and nations. One scholar shared her experiences in an Indian village, where she arrived shortly after a dowry-related murder. She spoke of the radical action women in the village took to prevent murders such as this from happening in the future and giving women a voice in community leadership. What was the radical change women wanted? They called for "eliminating violence against women, providing their community with access to health care, increasing educational opportunities for women and girls, and strengthening women's political influence."[8]

Development and aid work across the world have long proven that investing resources in women provides a more significant impact, even than investing in men, on a community. It's called the *multiplier effect*. For every dollar a woman earns, she makes a more substantial contribution to her family's health, education, and well-being than for every dollar a man earns. Therefore, investing in a woman is a direct investment in improving the lives of her entire family. In fact, one study showed that when women's income increased, the family invested more in food and less on alcohol and cigarettes.[9]

One study showed that "investment in women's education and health, and attention to their employment opportunities and empowerment, pays big dividends in terms of economic development."[10] Another showed that when women's security needs are met—through land ownership, equitable family law, reduction in violence against women, and so on—nations are more secure. Investment in women results in greater physical and financial security on macro- and microlevels.

Can you imagine a stabler, healthier, safer, and more financially secure world? We can, and it starts with women. Improving women's work opportunities is not only a case for gender equality, but it is also a case for increasing the flourishing of all. As Melinda Gates, founder of the Bill & Melinda Gates Foundation, which has made investments in women's health and prosperity across the world, put it in *The Moment of Lift,* "Because when you lift up women, you lift up humanity."[11]

WHY INVEST IN MARGINALIZED WOMEN?

Taking that a step further, our focus is specifically on women who have historically been marginalized. Women in this book experienced the intersectionality of their gender, class, and in some cases, race as they overcame poverty, incarceration, and addiction. Why focus on women our society has marginalized? You might be surprised to learn it is not because we think they need your help the most. It's because we believe *you* need *them* the most. The world needs them the most. In our work, we have met the most amazing women who overcame significant challenges. Through the stories and principles throughout this book, we show how women who are overcomers can have a positive impact on your organizations. They bring a unique skill set born from their experiences, not despite them. And they have created a unique future, solved tough problems, and persevered when others would have quit.

In addition to you needing these women, the overall economy needs them. A significant impact can be made by engaging

Arising from rock bottom is powerful.

all women in the economy and not just those with traditional pasts and affluent families. We have seen women go from living on the streets to being pillars of their community. Arising from rock bottom is powerful. Leaving them out is harmful. As Melinda Gates wrote,

> Saving lives starts with bringing everyone in. Our societies will be healthiest when they have no outsiders. We should strive for that. We have to keep working to reduce poverty and disease. We have to help outsiders resist the power of people who want to keep them out. But we have to do our inner work as well: We have to wake up to the ways we exclude. We have to open our arms and our hearts to the people we've

pushed to the margins. It's not enough to help outsiders fight their way
in—the real triumph will come when we no longer push anyone out.[12]

In what ways are we letting our own biases push others out—others
who don't look like us, who have had challenges out of their control,
and who have gone on a different path due to choices and circumstance? What can we do differently?

HOW TO INVEST WELL?

This book was born out of both personal experience and professional
research. The stories we are excited to share with you are those of
the women from the housing program where Cheryl worked, which
Shannon researched.[13] Women came to the housing program at the
darkest time in their lives when some combination of terrible circum-
stances and bad life choices led them into places of utter destruction
and desolation. The program supported women, and their children, in
any crisis situation. Over the years, the women most often served were
those who battled long-term addiction and multiple incarcerations.
Women arrived at the home of their own accord or through a referral
from another organization or social service agency. Others came to
the home as a condition of parole or probation. The program provided
permanent supportive housing, where women stayed nine months to
a year on average. Most arrived with little or no resources or support
after years of burning bridges with friends and family.

Despite the odds, maybe even because of the odds, the women
found the resilience, courage, and tenacity to claw their way into a
new future. And not just any future, mind you, but a future that can at
times be described as miraculous and impossible. The voices of these
powerful women demonstrate the effective principles introduced in
this book.

Through Shannon's research, it was clear the women from Cheryl's
housing program in South Texas were experiencing a dramatic transformation. The questions were *why* and *how*? The answer is the
six principles in this book, which Cheryl, along with her staff and
the women in the housing program, developed. The processes and

programs of the organization emerged organically. Staff worked daily to provide opportunities for women who wanted change and were ready to try. Some ideas and methods worked very well and some bombed big time.

It was evident that the program was successful in helping women transition to independent, healthy lifestyles. Over and over, women made the shift from poverty, addiction, incarceration, or engagement in the sex industry to obtain stable employment and housing as well as becoming able to provide for their families. If that was all that was accomplished, it would be powerful and significant considering the highly dysfunctional lifestyles that often spanned decades that participants led. Many did obtain that healthy life, but more remarkably, they also continued to do more than ever imagined. They earned high school, college, and graduate degrees, got sober, built careers, and even started counseling programs to service the populations from which they came. The results continue to have ripple effects.

As staff saw this incredible transformation in women's lives, they hungered to understand what was happening. What were the critical principles, processes, tools, and concepts that created this environment for radical change? We know that understanding and being able to explain how the transformation came about increases the ability to make it happen again or repeat the behavior. Over time, the principles that best supported women were refined into those presented here.

This book tells the stories of the most resilient, real people we know. These stories provide opportunities to move the needle on the challenges facing businesses today. Each story, however, is a kaleidoscope of many stories from people we have met over the years. No one single person is represented in each story. The reason we chose not to tell any one person's story is because we believe those stories belong to the person who experienced them. If individuals feel comfortable sharing their stories, we think it is their place to share their specific journey. If they choose not to share their stories, then we believe it is not our place to do so. To protect their individual stories, we treated the experiences, personalities, and conversations from the women in the past like ingredients for a cake. We poured them all into a bowl and mixed them up. When the cake was done, each piece represented a new, merged story from ingredients provided by many different women. When the real women we have encountered read the stories, they may recognize little pieces of themselves in a character but they will also recognize little pieces of other women they know.

Although the characters in a sense are fictional, all the successes, dramatic changes, unique perspectives, and even language belongs to at least one of the women from the program in South Texas. Most of the dialogue and thoughts occurred in real life of one of these real women. So, although the characters are fictional in their merging of personalities, the experiences and accomplishments are indeed real. All the names and identifying information of the individuals and companies, including industries, have been changed.

We refer to the women in different ways throughout this book. Their stories and their pasts are complicated, and they overcame issues like generational poverty, situational poverty, incarceration, domestic violence, sex trafficking, substance use, homelessness, and more. The same woman may be an offender and a survivor. So, a single term to reference the women we are writing about is virtually impossible. Sometimes we use the word *survivor*. Other times we use phrases like, women who have overcome challenging pasts or women overcomers. No matter what term we use, the women represented in these stories are our heroes.

We have learned a great deal through experience and research. We want to share that with you through the stories of the amazing women we have encountered. We hope using stories allows for deeper learning and connection.

When we talk about the women who have overcome challenging pasts, we are sharing a possible new future. We are talking about women who went from "turning tricks" to transforming communities as business leaders, counselors, and employees. When we say historically marginalized women, we are talking about women who have been through some horrific experiences and challenges. The stories primarily focus on the women's many successes and victories. However, we also tell some of the stories about the women's pasts. These stories may be challenging for some to read because they include experiences of domestic violence, sex trafficking, discrimination, harassment, and sexual abuse.

Most women in business experience a level of marginalization. But the women's stories we tell start with generational poverty and addiction in addition to more widespread challenges, like the gender pay gap. If some women can overcome living on the streets, multiple trips to prison, and breaking cycles of addiction and abuse, then we can all overcome the challenges we face in business today. If we can engage women like those in these stories in the fight, then they will do the overcoming with us.

The best part of what we have learned from the women captured in these stories is the ability to replicate these concepts in other contexts. Initially, the women were exposed to the principles in the book in a nonprofit setting. But all the women took the skills learned in that context and applied them as they entered the business world. This translation of concepts did not only apply to their journey as they worked in the world of business, but they also used these ideas to impact the business world.

As you read the stories, you will uncover profound yet straightforward ideas and tools to use in your business. As each story unfolds, we will take breaks to unpack the guiding principles at work that make these transformations a reality. Each chapter contains a story with interwoven explanations of the guiding principle revealed. We hope you are not only inspired by the amazing stories of the women but that you also glean the rich principles behind the words. However, we also need to address the challenges these guiding principles present. Yes, there are challenges in rethinking our traditional methods, but the risk is far less than the payoff in the end, as you will see as the stories conclude. And by addressing these challenges up front and providing solutions to overcome them, we're confident that all businesses can ultimately succeed in putting these principles to work in empowering marginalized women through their organizations.

Without a doubt, businesses that follow and implement these concepts and tools will see an increase in effective corporate responsibility. But even more exciting are the positive impacts the women will have on the business internally. Working with women like those in this book is as great an asset to the business world as it is to the women and their families. Women overcomers represent so many others who are intelligent, courageous, and tenacious overcomers.

They are women who become employees and leaders that will bring increased sales, revenue, and impact through all levels of business. What a win-win! You will learn how to structure your business to make a difference in the world. The women who are given opportunities by businesses like yours will transform their lives and their wider communities. And your business will reap the benefits of employing these high-impact, innovative leaders, setting them up for success.

1

DON'T BLINK!

Experiential Learning

Don't blink. Don't blink, she repeated to herself over and over, as if not blinking would be the dam stopping the flood of tears threatening to streak her perfect makeup.

Cara had been invited to a power breakfast for the new team charged with the task of creating McMillan International's social responsibility program. She was thrilled the CEO had selected her to chair the task force. This breakfast meeting was going to launch the new initiative. The guest speaker was David Whitte, one of the authors of the popular book *Overcoming Poverty*. Cara had read the book and was familiar with realities of the poor at the heart of the book's message.

Everything was going smoothly until Whitte spoke about the marred identity of the poor. With each new insight he discussed, Cara's heartbeat increased. His words rang true. Poverty was her reality twenty years ago when she first walked through the doors of McMillan International. Her past experience as a poor single mother had indeed marred her identity. And because of that, she was still trying to prove to the world she was somebody. She thought back to the day she arrived at the regional office for her interview.

In fall 1988, Cara was a single mother with two children younger than age three. The day her second child was born she vowed to do anything and everything to provide her children with a future. At the time, that meant taking classes at the local college, working part-time at a call center, living with her best friend to save money, and doing whatever she could to not lose her $359 from Aid to Families with Dependent Children (AFDC).

Even with AFDC, WIC, and food stamps, Cara could not make ends meet. So, she also worked two nights a week dancing topless at the Starlight Club. She hated dancing, but the tips weren't reported, which meant she could keep her AFDC. Every time she walked through the club's doors shame washed over her. She prayed her children would never know, but for now, they needed formula and diapers, and she needed money to pay doctor bills.

One requirement for Cara's welfare checks was her commitment to work with a local nonprofit called Building Futures. They provided one thing she needed desperately: daycare. But they also required her to participate in job preparedness classes, and the last thing Cara wanted was one more thing to do. Besides, she was sure it was nothing more than do-gooder church ladies who would make her feel like crap.

Despite her skepticism, Cara went to Building Futures—even though she was convinced they would see her as a project, the poor single mom needing to be "fixed." At her first appointment, she was assigned a caseworker, Alicia, who took Cara down the hall to see the daycare center. It was amazing. Everything was so bright and clean.

After going over all the policies and signing the necessary paperwork, Cara turned to Alicia. "Okay, what the hell do I do now?" Cussing always rattled the church ladies, so she was sure to throw it in there for good measure.

But Cara was caught off guard when Alicia replied, "I don't know. What the hell do you want to do? This is your life to make or ruin, not mine."

That was different. For the first time, Cara really didn't have an answer—genuine or sarcastic. She started to list some of the struggles of her past, trying to shock Alicia, but the case worker just nodded. "Yup, me too." Alicia explained she had been where Cara was five years ago. *Five years!* Cara thought. *My kids will be in school in five years.* But sitting there looking at Alicia, poised, well-dressed, and confident, she saw a glimpse of a different woman she could become. By the end of the meeting, her kids were enrolled in day-care and she was signed up for a course called Business Professional Academy (BPA).

After successfully graduating from BPA, Cara was sent on her first professional interview. Going to that first interview was difficult. She repeated to herself what Alicia told her at every meeting. *You can do this. You've got this.* Alicia told her to stop focusing on what she couldn't do and focus on what she could.

The morning of the interview, she opened the doors to the regional office of McMillan International. The air from the window units was a stark contrast to the heat that had almost melted her on the way from her car to the door. She had parked in the back of the lot so no one would see the sun-damaged paint and missing bumper. She'd bought the car that way and was proud of it at the time. *It's mine. I did this,* she thought. But she soon realized the car told the world that she didn't have enough and that she wasn't good enough.

Trying to show confidence that she did not really have, Cara walked briskly up to the reception desk.

"I am here to see . . ." she began, panicking as she fumbled for the name of the man she was there to meet.

"Mr. Cannon," she finally blurted.

The receptionist smiled. "Take a seat. Jon will be right with you." As Cara sat, she rubbed her hands on her pants to make sure there was no sweat in case Mr. Cannon tried to shake hands. She could time it just right to make sure the sweat was gone before she grabbed his hand.

A voice snapped her out of her thoughts. "You must be Cara. I'm Jon Cannon."

Instantly his hand was out to greet her. Wiping her hand on her pants now would make her look like an idiot. Embarrassed, she shoved her sweaty, shaking palm into his.

"Yes, I am. Nice to meet you, Mr. Cannon."

"Jon, please, call me Jon," he said in a friendly tone, leading her into his office.

The interview was nothing Cara expected. At BPA, they practiced interview questions, but Mr. Cannon was not asking any of the questions she rehearsed. Several times, she fumbled over her answers and gave herself a mental lashing.

With support from Alicia, Cara had done her research. The company did $500 million in revenue internationally. Cara was interviewing at one of their field offices, but it was still a big deal. The company was big time, with good benefits. She was terrified of losing this chance.

To close the interview, Mr. Cannon asked Cara about her goals for the future. Cara was caught completely off guard.

She finally replied, "Right now, all I want is to get this job."

Mr. Cannon thanked her for coming in, and she left. As soon as she got in her car, negative self-talk flooded her mind. *I can't believe how stupid I sounded. There is no way they will hire me. What was I thinking? Who am I to try to work in an office job?* When Cara went to the interview, she knew the odds weren't good. After fumbling through the interview, she was back in Alicia's office crying that it was never going to work.

And then, miraculously, it did. She was shocked when two weeks later she got a call asking if she was still interested. The following week she was an administrative assistant in a McMillan field office. It took her six months to finally call Mr. Cannon "Jon" despite his persistence in correcting her.

From her new perch at the reception desk, Cara was the first face people met when applying for a job in their region. She greeted new applicants and connected them with the correct interviewer. It didn't take long to pick out the individuals not likely to be hired. She realized early on that she had much to learn if she wanted to remain employed. The more she watched her coworkers, the more she realized that she did not have the same professional skills and appearance. Although Jon tried not to let it show, it was clear he got frustrated with her.

One morning, Jon placed some notes on Cara's desk. "I need you to create meeting agendas for the next quarter and send to the team with these details by this afternoon."

Cara looked startled. "I've never done an agenda, Mr. Cannon. Can you show me what you mean?" she asked.

Jon shook his head brusquely. "Cara, you're on your own on this one. I'm out for the afternoon. You're smart; figure it out."

And with that he was gone. Her stomach twisted as she realized she had no idea what to do. She went to her computer and googled how to create an agenda. *Why was she so stupid? How could she work in an office and not know how to write an agenda?* But two hours later, the agenda was complete, and Cara felt incredible.

That was the day she realized she was smart.

EXPERIENTIAL LEARNING

Cara's story beautifully reveals the first guiding principle that equips businesses to do good: create an experiential, or discovery-based, learning model.

What Is Experiential Learning?

Information and knowledge can be disseminated or discovered. There is a place for both methods of teaching and learning. Most job-readiness programs are structured with a traditional didactic learning format: the teacher presents the information and the students listen and apply the information given. In a traditional classroom setting, the instructor still commonly presents information through lecture and the learner plays a passive role. The teacher is the only person tasked with the dissemination of ideas.

However, we now have enough data to show passive learning is not effective in traditional education[1] or in workplace education.[2] One of the primary challenges in learning is transference of knowledge.[3] Our brains naturally struggle with applying information learned in one setting to another setting. We advise students in traditional classroom settings to test in the same seat they learned the material because even moving across the room can make information recall challenging. Imagine the challenge of transferring information to a new job or a new company. Practice, or application, helps us overcome issues with transference by helping our brain make more solid connections representative of an expert rather than a novice.[4]

Experiential learning can exist without a teacher as it relates to the meaning-making process of the individual's direct experiences.[5] Humans are meaning-making machines. We are constantly trying to understand what and why things happen around us. When tasked with a job outside our understanding or experiences, we begin the search to determine what the task requires and means. In doing so, new meaning is created where none existed prior to the process.

> *Humans are meaning-making machines.*

Aristotle wrote, "For the things we have to learn before we can do them, we learn by doing them." We learn to ride a bicycle by riding a bicycle. We learn how to draw by drawing. This concept is relevant in more areas than we realize. In most businesses, we learn by doing in on-the-job training. We figure it out as we go. Yet in formal employee-training programs, experiential learning is significantly underused.

Requirements for Experiential Learning

For this guiding principle to work well, there are several elements that are necessary. First and foremost is time. This method of learning is most often *initially* more time-consuming. If employees do not have a specific skill or insight, allowing them time to learn on their own or search out possible answers is a must. The employees will retain the answer more effectively than if told the answer by a supervisor. The initial time investment made in experiential learning is worth the ultimate payoff of the employee's rapid improvement.

> *The initial time investment made in experiential learning is worth the ultimate payoff of the employee's rapid improvement.*

However, unlimited time to figure out a task or answer is not necessary or even beneficial in all cases. When Jon tasked Cara with creating meeting agendas, he gave her a deadline to have them out by the afternoon. Although there was a time limit, there was still enough time to allow her to discover the information on her own, which she did. What is important is to allow enough time for the task assigned. Jon knew it would only take a few Google searches and Cara could find templates for meeting agendas. Later in Cara's story, as her projects expand, so will the time Jon gives her to complete them. It can become an art to know how much time to allow for learning, that is, when to put deadlines and when not.

It is also necessary to have adequate resources. Access to Internet either through computer or smart devices is necessary when tasking staff with learning a new skill independently. Are there specific policies that shape business protocol? If so, would these policies be a beneficial resource when employees experiment with new products or processes? It is also necessary to have the space both in time and logistics to search and explore new ideas or learn tasks independently. Is there time in the schedule to allow for learning? Is there an area in the work setting where employees can sit and search for information?

When using experiential learning, it is important to set clear expectations and parameters. In Cara's story, Jon assigned the task of creating an agenda. He gave her clear directions. He wanted meeting agendas for the next quarter. He wanted them sent to the team by the afternoon. And even though we don't know what they are, he did give her details to include. With that clarity, Cara was able to take the time needed and accomplish exactly what was required.

Reflective observation is a critical component of experiential learning.[6] Reflection can occur after completing a task or while completing a task. "Reflection-on" is defined as reflecting on an experience or task after it is completed. "Reflection-in" is defined as reflection while completing a task.[7] Supervisors who support employees' reflection may see better results in employee learning.

Feedback is a great way to foster reflection. Feedback is different from instruction in that it starts with something the employees have already learned independently. Use feedback to help with quality control. Not all tasks completed through experiential learning are perfect the first time around. It may require several trips back to the drawing table to produce the best quality. But feedback should be constructive, open, and again, include clear parameters for what is expected or what is not necessary.

We encourage supervisors using experiential learning to provide employees with direct feedback and ask them questions that will support their reflection on such feedback. For example, in every meeting with her staff, Shannon provides reflection questions, which include:

- What did we do well as a team this week?
- What could we have done better? What processes need to change as a result?
- What is our objective for the coming week?

Such questions provide the team an opportunity to reflect on what everyone could have done better and what they could have done better as a team. Asking an employee these questions on a more microlevel helps as well. For example,

- What went well with this task?
- What could have been done better? What processes need to change for the outcome to be better next time?
- What is our objective for this task the next time you complete it?

Providing employees with a consistent framework of questions they can expect in an after-action review will help them with reflection-in action. They will start to reflect while they are completing a task and not just when the task is over. Reflection and constructive feedback can provide exponential benefits as tasks are repeated.

The final requirement for this principle is autonomy. Employees must be given autonomy to work independently. Employees must also understand when it is expected they work autonomously. This is not limited to a single individual. Autonomy can be given to work teams as well. The main thing is that if the individual or team is given a task that is to be developed through experiential learning, then they must be left alone and allowed to work. This seems logical, but it is not always natural. Managers and mentors have to resist the urge to step in and give hints or point an experiential learner in a certain direction. When we already know how to do something, it is natural to want to share that knowledge. And, of course, there are places where sharing insights is highly valuable and should be used. But we should not share our knowledge when we are tasking others to learn through discovery.

Creating an Experiential Learning Environment

If experiential learning is underused, how do we begin to create spaces in our current work environment for this principle? And what elements need to be in place? Once a business decides to use this principle, the first step is to evaluate the different areas of work and production that could create a learning lab for employees. An easy starting place is to identify where this principle will not work. The following questions can help eliminate tasks or processes that will not lend themselves well to this concept.

- What areas of work are limited by significant time constraints?
- What tasks or processes have set parameters that must be adhered to or followed?
- What tasks cannot withstand trial and error?
- What tasks or processes must follow specific governmental policies or regulations?

A business that works with chemicals, for example, would not want employees learning experientially how to prepare the products. Most likely, each chemical has specific ingredients that cannot be varied. Any task with a short deadline would also not be a good fit for experiential learning.

In the same way, the following questions can identify areas that are open for exploring and learning.

- Are there daily activities that can be learned through discovery as opposed to training?
- What recurring tasks are important for someone to learn and repeat?
- What tasks can be corrected through internal review before sharing with anyone outside the organization?

Tasks related to a more in-depth knowledge of software programs are an excellent space for experiential learning. An employee may come to the job with basic knowledge of Adobe InDesign. An assignment requiring more advanced knowledge of the software can be learned experientially because there are countless resources and tutorials online to learn advanced elements of the program.

Each business will have to explore and experiment with different areas of work and processes to determine which allow for discovery. This approach may seem costly and time-consuming. And it's true that taking valuable work time to explore all areas of a business that work with experiential learning would distract from the core profit-generating processes. Instead, start with one area and explore what tasks and processes work well. Once that area has been developed with success, move on to another.

When businesses decide to implement the experiential learning principle, there must be open communication with all that will be impacted. If this approach has never been used, employees and managers need to know a shift is coming. A great starting place would be to communicate with all employees and create a team to develop the areas that will be implemented. Allow the team to develop the communication that will be sent to others on how the concept will be implemented in your work setting. Allowing those impacted by these principles the opportunity to explore how this will work in your business creates buy-in. It is the employees that are most impacted by using this principle, so it makes sense for them to develop the protocol and expectation and then communicate to the remaining teams or staff.

CARA CONTINUES TO THRIVE

About a year into her employment, Cara was sitting in the monthly staff meeting taking notes. One of the directors voiced frustration about turnover among personnel out in the field. They discussed concerns that pay was the reason people left, but Cara wasn't sure she agreed.

After the meeting, she decided to approach Jon. Somewhat timidly she tapped on his door. He waved her in and as she sat, she began to explain her thoughts. In her role as the receptionist, she had talked to hundreds of people applying for those positions. They wanted a fair wage, sure, but those positions came with competitive salaries. Cara suspected loyalty was the reason—loyalty from the company to the employee as much as from the employee to the company.

Cara spent a lot of time that first year watching people as they came seeking employment. She felt appearance often mattered more than ability. It is hard in a thirty-minute interview to look past the biases that come with a messy exterior. Yet, she had a feeling the directors did not hire a few people with raw talent. It's hard to identify potential, but Cara had an idea.

"Do you think I am a good employee?" Cara asked.

"No. I think you are an exceptional employee," Jon replied.

She went on to explain that she thought the company was missing out on some potentially loyal employees because of their interview style. Many of the women seeking employment reminded her of herself when she started. She didn't know all their backstories, but she noticed telltale signs they were similar—slightly inappropriate clothing or the street lingo they used while chatting before the interview. And Cara knew if they were like her, they wouldn't do well with the company's current interview process. Cara suggested revamping the office's hiring practices to consider individuals who were less "traditional" candidates. They could include problem-solving assessments to supplement the behavioral interviews the company currently performed. That would allow them to gain deeper insight into possible untapped potential of the candidates.

Then, she added, if they did choose to use a different hiring approach, they would also have to develop a different training approach.

Jon loved the idea and made the project Cara's new assignment. He didn't give her a time frame but asked her to put together all the details for his review. As Cara walked back to her desk, that grumble in her stomach started again. She had never expected to have to *create* the program. How was she to know what to do? She considered turning around to go back in to say, *never mind*, but then she stopped. It was her idea. She was smart; she could do it.

Two weeks later, Jon leafed through her new interview process and training program. Reading quietly, Jon began to grin on page two. With each page turn he either let out a small laugh or nodded his head.

Finally, he said, "This is incredible. I am impressed. Schedule a team meeting for Friday so you can present this to everyone."

Cara didn't know if she wanted to celebrate or throw up. It was beyond exciting that the company was going to use her program . . . but presenting to the other staff? Yet, that Friday, dressed in her soft grey blouse hanging loosely over her tailored black slacks, Cara presented the program.

Within a month, there were four women hired using the new policies. Cara led the training program and created a space where the women felt free to asks questions and share concerns. The group became close quickly. They didn't all work in the same departments, so they rarely talked about issues that were specific to the job. Most of the conversations were about expectations, fears, and insecurities.

Several women expressed frustrations with the work environment in other departments. As Cara asked more questions, she realized that management in those departments did not share the same approach to supervising that Cara and Jon did. It became clear that the supervisors required some training as well. The supervisors also needed to be accountable for the program through metrics based on employees' performance and feedback from employees.

Cara took the idea of training supervisors across all departments to Jon, and he gave the green light. But the morning before she was to lead the first training, Cara found herself in the familiar place of mental wrestling, *What are you doing? These are supervisors.* As in the past, however, she pushed the thoughts aside and took charge. The response was incredible. She could see the expressions of the supervisors change when they seemed to get it.

Not everyone was on the same page because it soon became clear to Cara that not all of the supervisors thought this new approach would work. Two men in particular voiced their dissent.

Steve complained, "We've hired these people before. And when it was all said and done, they just didn't want to work."

Bob chimed in, "Exactly. And they are more interested in smoke breaks than work."

Cara was determined not to let that stop what she knew could work. She thanked Steve and Bob for their opinions but indicated that the new practices would go into effect—and that she believed the company would see results. And they did. At the end of the first twelve months, employee turnover had dropped from 30 percent to 7 percent. The news quickly spread to other regions and the program grew. At the end of the second year, Cara was promoted to human resources (HR) management at the regional office that came with a substantial raise. And even better, it came with a private office and the opportunity to hire her own assistant.

When Cara's new assistant started a week later, Cara filled her in on important topics that were not in the employee handbook, such as stupid comments. Cara told her of a comment a manager made once while staring at her chest, "Oh, nice dress. It really fits you well."

"I mean seriously," Cara asked, "do you ever hear women saying to a male employee, 'Oh nice slacks, they really fit you well.'" Of course, there are policies in place for sexual harassment that worked for obvious infractions. But they fell short in addressing subtle comments or crude jokes.

From time to time, Cara would give her assistant challenging work projects. She wanted her to experience opportunities to push herself. Sometimes the assistant pushed back. Cara would just smile and remind her she was smart and could figure it out. And every time, she did.

WHY EXPERIENTIAL LEARNING WORKS

There are many benefits to experiential learning. Employees can acquire many skills needed in the workplace through an experiential learning model.[8] Employers value skills like self-confidence, strong work ethic, problem-solving, flexibility, adaptability, and working well under pressure. Not all employees show up on the first day of work with those skill sets. Providing employees opportunities to learn through experience supports development of such skills.

Imagine the confidence Cara gained when she learned, independently, how to create a meeting agenda. For many, that task would not be a challenge at all, but it was outside Cara's experiences and it challenged her. This principle is not limited to working with nontraditional employees. Individuals that are allowed an opportunity to experiment and discover new ideas will gain confidence when they accomplish a task or learn new insights. Having employees that are confident in their ability to perform and impact the business has great potential to increase production and also profits.

The time Cara dedicated to learning how to make an agenda created a stronger work ethic, one motivated by the goal to succeed on even the smallest assignments. When teams and employees are given autonomy to learn new ideas and develop new processes, the freedom to do so creates the by-product of increasing work ethic. When working independently, as individuals or teams, the work required to accomplish the goal must come from within.

Like Cara, when employees are given a task that is outside their current knowledge, they need to search for information needed to complete that task. What makes this challenging is the idea of *you don't know what you don't know*. This requires creative thinking just to determine where to start. As information is gathered, new ideas begin to emerge and eventually the task is accomplished. All problem-solving starts in the same place: asking what information and tools do I need to solve this problem? Developing and increasing problem-solving abilities becomes an asset that is exponential. Not only will employees learn to solve problems in contexts where learning is being explored, but that skill will also flow over into other areas or work when problems arise. Teams or individuals that know they can solve problems will naturally flow into that process when problems arise.

It is easy to understand how learning through experiences or discovery can develop the skills of flexibility and adaptability. The trial and error involved with learning through this method forces the learner to adapt and try different approaches before discovering the solution. A problem facing many companies is a fixed mindset—represented by comments like "This is how we have always done things," which is a dangerous approach. Of course, there will always be areas that are highly effective and must be maintained. But many industries have been, or will be, impacted by technology. The hotel and motel industry now competes with companies like Airbnb and HomeAway. Brick-and-mortar bookstores have significantly diminished with the rise of Amazon. Barnes and Noble adapted to include both an online and brick-and-mortar presence where customers can not only purchase books but also coffee, food, and gifts. Customers find space to sit and read or meet with friends. Businesses that develop adaptable and flexible employees will position themselves to adapt and change as technology changes.

Cara's thoughts of *Why was I so stupid? How could I work in an office and not know how to write an agenda?* demonstrate the internal pressure that occurs when an employee does not know exactly how to accomplish a task. Every time Cara persevered despite her uncertainty, she developed skills that will be available to her in other high-pressure situations. This ties into the same concept of adaptability. With changes occurring rapidly and, at times, dramatically, the pressure increases to continually adapt and navigate those changes. Having leaders and team members that can operate under pressure is gold and not just for survival but also for continued growth.

As revealed in Shannon's research,[9] women trained through an experiential, or discovery-based learning, model realized they were capable of far more than they knew possible when they independently accomplished a task. The women Shannon interviewed frequently said the most valuable learning experiences they had was when a supervisor gave them a new task with little instruction. Cheryl's favorite lines referenced by participants were, "read books," "Google it," "look it up," "learn," and an all-time favorite: "figure it out."[10] One participant said she was particularly trying to rely on Cheryl to teach her how to create a mass e-mail. Finally, she went to go figure it out on her own when Cheryl responded to her complaints with, "Well, you've got all day to figure it out!"[11]

As successful leaders, we so frequently struggle with delegation, but delegation was critical to participants' development and confidence. A critical component of experiential learning is taking care to not assign a task the individual cannot figure out. This is different from assigning tasks an individual does not know they can figure out. The goal is to help the employee realize they can figure it out, even if they don't know how to do so yet. Discovery takes longer than telling, but the rewards are exponential in the time it saves by creating an independent employee in the long term. Through experiential learning one can shift their language and attitude from, "But, I don't know how" to "If I can do this, what else can I accomplish?"

The participants not only learned a skill, but they also learned how to push past obstacles. Rather than quitting when something was difficult, the women persevered when encouraged to keep seeking answers. This inspired a sense of pride they had never experienced. Those working with them were always quick to point out they had had that skill all along. For instance, when those in addiction are desperate to secure more drugs, they didn't give up when the first person they called had nothing for them. In that drug life, they pursued until they found the source of their next high. The ability to translate skills learned in difficult or negative life situations to positive work environments will be discussed further in chapter 4, where we dive into the "Translation Factor."

Experiential learning allows employees the opportunity to make productive mistakes that lead to innovation, increased knowledge, and productivity. Obviously, the women were not 100 percent successful the first time. The chance to redo a project several times created an environment in which not achieving perfection on the first attempt or even failure was okay.

Another important concept, related to experiential learning, is reducing miseducative experiences.[12] Miseducative experiences prevent someone from learning from an experience. For example, if Cara had been given a task too challenging for her current state of development, she might have been frustrated and quit. The frustration and discouragement someone may feel from a negative experience might prevent them from learning from the experience. Some experiences can interfere with, rather than contribute to, learning. Therefore, supervisors who plan to incorporate experiential learning as a means for developing their staff should exercise caution to ensure tasks aid learning and not interfere with such learning.

There are several strategies for minimizing miseducative experiences. In Cara's story, creating a meeting agenda seemed extremely challenging and unknown to her, but Jon knew the task was just beyond what Cara could do on her own. There are several important concepts at play here. The first concept is the zone of proximal development.[13] Learning for development is most effective when the learner is tasked with something just beyond their current skill set. Asking Cara to develop a business plan at this point in her career would have been beyond her reach and unrealistic. The gap in her knowledge likely would have caused her to freeze and not be able to complete the task at all. However, Jon assessed her abilities and knew she was capable of creating a meeting agenda, even though it was not something she presently knew how to do. The meeting agenda was within her zone of proximal development.

The company Yelp is an example of effectively implementing an experiential learning culture consistent with the zone of proximal development. According to James Balagot, head of Learning and Development for Yelp, the company hires employees into "stretch roles"[14]—roles just beyond an employee's current ability level. Yelp intends these roles to provide employees with learning experiences that will frequently challenge them, "accelerate their development," and help the company iterate more rapidly.[15]

Scaffolding[16] is another strategy a supervisor can adopt. Once Cara knew how to create a meeting agenda, her zone of proximal development expanded. There were more tasks within her reach. Scaffolding is a process of providing support that is gradually removed. It's unrealistic to expect people to reach the highest point of their job or learning without support. Gradually taking away support or gradually increasing the difficulty of the task scaffolds or provides a supportive base for an employee's development. Jon provided scaffolding for Cara by giving her support when needed and gradually removing the support as Cara become more capable. As Jon continued to give her more challenging tasks she was ready to accomplish them at that point in her career, but when she was first learning to complete a meeting agenda those more challenging tasks would have been too difficult.

One of the best benefits of experiential learning is that it creates lasting behavior. Once you learn to ride a bike, you always know how to ride a bike. You may get rusty if you don't ride often. But it only takes a few tries, and you are right back to being a bike rider. In the workplace, experiential learning becomes an excellent building block to increase employee skill and eventually increase efficiency and revenue. Once an individual learns a new skill through experiential learning, that behavior remains consistent and creates a foundation for the next skill set to be built upon. Eventually, the employees become highly proficient at learning and adapting. A highly proficient workforce can create highly efficient outputs.

CARA'S NEXT CHALLENGE

The following year, McMillan closed a significant acquisition when they purchased a struggling competitor. Cara played a critical role in the acquisition as the Chief Human Resources Officer (CHRO)—a role she took after a big promotion. The investment bank that facilitated the deal took the executives to a celebratory lunch at Foster's Steakhouse. Cara hated Foster's because it was across the street from Twilight Gentleman's Club. Cara rode with Frank McIntyre, CEO, C. J. Mallory, CFO, and Tom Gaston, COO. She was the lone female among the executives.

As they pulled up, Tom nudged his elbow into C. J.'s side as he nodded his head toward the Twilight and softly said, "Maybe we owe you a lap dance for getting this deal done."

C. J. responded back, "Not from those dirty bitches."

Tom and C. J.'s conversation was quiet, but everyone in the group heard. Frank looked embarrassed but just chose to ignore it. Red patches popped up on Cara's cheeks and neck. She kept repeating in her mind, *stay calm, stay calm.* The men certainly didn't know her history working as a topless dancer. Still, she felt sure her facial expression would give away her secret.

Getting out of the car, she started for the restaurant. Walking with eyes down, she focused on her classy pumps—the expensive ones she worked hard to buy. The realization of all her hard work stopped her. She spun around to face the men.

"Can someone please explain to me why the women in that place"—she jerked her thumb toward the club—"are referred to as bitches, but the men who drool over them are called gentlemen? Or better yet, can someone explain why the two of you think it is appropriate to say something like that in the first place?" she fired out.

C. J. and Tom began back peddling and apologizing, making them look like bigger jerks. Cara fumed, but no one else spoke up. The rest of their group had joined them by now, but everyone averted their eyes and kept walking toward the steakhouse.

By the time the food arrived, things appeared to settle down and the incident forgotten. Cara tried to enjoy lunch, but she could not calm down. Her emotions flipped from rage that the comment was not addressed, to disgust with C. J. and Tom, and then to shame because she had been one of "those" women.

She remembered so many men like C. J. and Tom. The thought of their eyes and lust made her skin crawl. All her hard work and men still thought they could say those things. Maybe today they'd thought of her as one of the guys in the car, or maybe they hadn't even registered her presence. Either way, she felt diminished.

When they got back to the building, everyone went their separate ways. Cara sat in her office, elbows on her desk and face buried in her hands. She was the head of HR. She couldn't ignore this, but the men had more power than she did.

A knock bolted her from her thoughts. It was Jon. He had been in the corporate offices for a meeting that morning and ran into Frank after lunch.

"McIntyre told me what happened," Jon said.

"Okay," said Cara uncertainly. "So, what happens from here?"

Jon said, "It's kind of up to you. I assume you will put a memo in their files and the incident will be a part of their next reviews." *Like that will amount to anything,* Cara thought.

"More importantly, do you want to talk?" he asked.

Something in his tone caused Cara's throat to tighten. "Jon, I used to be one of those women."

His wide eyes and dropped jaw made it clear he never suspected she had worked in a strip club. Cara went on to explain that most of the women working at his regional office were women she knew from her past. Again, Jon was floored.

Finally, he said, "I'm proud of you, Cara. You and the others have overcome a lot despite your past."

Cara shook her head. "You just don't get it. We are not good employees despite our past. We are good employees *because* of our past," she responded.

The very things they needed to survive that life were the skills that made them incredible employees. She asked him if he ever worked part-time, went to school full-time, and worked two nights a week in the pit of hell, all while raising two babies alone. Of course, he hadn't. She continued. The skills that allowed them to survive their past were the exact skills companies expected of employees: hard work, figuring things out, and hustle. The entire premise behind the project she created was to show other nontraditional employees, especially women like her, that they were capable. They just needed to teach employees with sketchy backgrounds that they already had the skills and that they had just been using them in the wrong way.

"*Those* women were not the women most companies would be seeking to hire," she said.

He smiled. "And yet you hired them."

It was her turn to smile back. "Yes, I did. And if this company doesn't recognize their value, someone else will and it will be a loss for us."

Most people never knew about Cara's past, but after the incident a few did, including McIntyre. Knowing her backstory along with the significant work she had done led him to reassess the corporation's responsibility to the employees and the community. And that led to the creation of the CRS Task Force that Cara was the chair of and several of the women were members.

It had also been McIntyre's idea to bring in Whitte to launch this new initiative. Of course, Jon was there as well that morning. So, sitting at breakfast, Cara struggled. Whitte's words were true. The deep scars from her past still had not completely healed. Because of that, she was still trying to show the world she was somebody. Trying desperately not to cry, out of the corner of her eye she saw Jon move closer.

Leaning in he whispered, "It's okay to cry."

He was right. He knew her story in all its triumphs, challenges, and ugliness. Looking down at the half-eaten bagel smeared with cream cheese, she set her mind. Yes, she had scars. However, no longer would she try to prove what was already true. She was smart. No, not just smart; she was brilliant. With that the tears flowed freely as, finally, she blinked.

2

I LOVE YOU FOREVER

Immediate Leadership Opportunities

"I love you forever. Forever and always. To the moon and back my sweet baby girl," whispered Rosalinda as she lay on the floor.

There was no one to hear those words. But Rosalinda didn't care. In her mind she was in her old house sitting next to Carrie, tucking her into bed. That was years ago, but Rosalinda's love had not faded. She loved her children even though she was no longer raising them. Her sister took the children after Child Protective Services (CPS) removed them from her home because of her husband George's violence. If only CPS could have removed Rosalinda as well. But they didn't, and here she was again.

Blood seeped from her nose and lip onto the gray sheets spotted with brown and yellow stains. Rosalinda curled in the fetal position and dared not move. She lay completely still, hoping George was so drunk he would pass out. But instead, he grabbed her by the hair, pulled her up, and smashed the side of her face into the door frame. The impact caused something to crack, causing an explosion of lights in Rosalinda's eyes, and was so powerful that Rosalinda's legs crumpled. As she began to fall, George was furious and screamed at her to stand up. No matter how hard she tried her mind could not convince her legs to work. As she continued to fall, she felt the steel toe of his boot slam into her side. She wasn't sure how many times he kicked her while she lay on the floor. All the while he thundered, "Get up, you whore!"

When the kicking stopped, Rosalinda grabbed the edge of the bed and tried to pull herself up. George decided to help and grabbed her by the throat and shoved her face down onto the bed. Digging both knees into her back, George grabbed Rosalinda's head and began to twist while still holding her down with his knees. Rosalinda panicked. He twisted her neck so far; she knew it was about to snap and she was about to die.

Then in an instant he was off her screaming, "You want to be a whore, I will show you what happens to whores," as he ripped off her pants.

She could hear him undressing and knew what was coming. There was nothing she could do. Any attempt to stop her husband would only lead to a more severe beating. After he finished, he jumped up and began shuffling around the room with his pants around his ankles mumbling. Every now and then she could make out a word or phrase: *whore, idiot, who does she think she is?*

Eventually, the door slammed, and she heard the thump of George falling onto the couch. But even then, she didn't budge. It was only when she heard the deep growl of his snore that she began to stir. Weakly, she pushed up on her elbows trying to get up. Just that small movement sent her mind into a swirl, forcing her to remain still until the spinning stopped. After a few minutes, she sat up. She didn't need to go to the bathroom mirror to know she looked bad. One eye was already almost completely closed from where it met the doorframe. She could taste blood as she touched each tooth gently with her tongue to see if they were still intact.

She hated this life. All she had done that night was smoke the last joint she had. George always had plenty dope because he was one of the local dealers. How was she to know he was out as well. As she lay on her back, tears rolled down her cheeks. She desperately wanted out, but she had long since stopped dreaming of being rescued. What felt even more desperate was no one even knew she needed saving. The only people around her were other crack addicts, and they just chalked it up to the life. Finally, she drifted off to sleep wrapped in hopelessness.

As usual, Rosalinda went nowhere until the red blotches turned deep purple, slowly faded to yellow and disappeared. George acted like nothing happened, like her swollen face was not real. She hated him. She loved him. Without George, she would be forced to sleep on the streets. As horrible as his rages could be, at least she had a bed to sleep in, and not to mention, dope to ease the pain.

Two weeks later life was back to normal. One of her jobs for George was to hit the local food pantries around town. She would keep the few items they liked, Spam, Rice-a-Roni, and Stove Top stuffing. The rest she would take to the convenience store on the corner. The manager, Alfred, would buy the food she didn't want. He would buy it cheaper from her than he could from his vendors. Then he would turn around and put it on his shelf to sell it and make a bigger profit. It was a perfect deal for everybody. Rosalinda got money to help with bills, Alfred made more money, and the do-gooders at the church food pantries got to feel good about helping poor little Rosalinda. Win. Win. Win.

When Rosalinda walked into Alfred's Sac 'n' Pac with her goods, she ran into Angela. Rosalinda and Angela smoked dope together all the time. But seeing her here now, Rosalinda realized she hadn't seen her in a while. Angela finished paying for her soda and bag of chips. When she turned to leave, her eyes met Rosalinda's.

"Rosie, girl, how have you been?" she smiled and asked.

Rosie is what her close friends called her. She replied, "Oh you know, just same ole same ole. Where have you been?"

Angela went on to explain she moved in with a friend and decided she was tired of the life. She spent several weeks detoxing—several horrible, miserable weeks. But when she came out of the fog and cramps, she had time to think about what she wanted. Someone told her about a new program at a local church. They helped people figure out how to get good jobs or start their own businesses. Angela went on to say she went through that program, and they gave her a loan to start her taco business, Uno, Dos, Tacos.

"You should check them out, it is *way* better than that life," Angela said, as her eyes dropped to the bags Rosalinda carried.

Rosalinda just stood staring at Angela with her mouth open. Finally, she came out of her daze of embarrassment and congratulated

Angela. She also said she wasn't sure she had what it took to do what Angela was doing. They stood there and talked a little while longer. Finally, Angela left and said to text her if she changed her mind. Rosalinda met Alfred in the back office, got her cash, and headed back home. But she couldn't stop thinking about Angela.

Every day Rosalinda thought about Angela. *If she can do it maybe I can, too.* Then she would convince herself differently. *That's stupid. I can't do that. I'm not smart enough. Those people probably wouldn't want me in their program.* On and on she went giving herself every excuse as to why she couldn't get out like Angela had. But every single day she thought about it—every single day!

Eventually, she mustered up the courage to text Angela. She texted and asked if she was still willing to help her find out about the program. Immediately Angela texted back that she would. She even told her she would come pick her up in an hour, give her a ride, and go with her. Rosalinda was caught off guard. She didn't expect to go that day. She looked like shit. She tried to make excuses, but Angela kept texting and telling her she could do it. Finally, Rosalinda agreed. She jumped in the shower—at least she would wash her hair. She pulled on the cleanest shirt and shorts she could find and waited until Angela texted that she was outside.

Thirty minutes later, Rosalinda walked through the doors of the Innovation Station. The woman behind the desk saw Angela and jumped up and hugged her. Angela explained that Rosie was interested in taking classes at the Station. With great enthusiasm, the woman took them down the hall to meet the coordinator, Ellen Graves. All the smiles and enthusiasm seemed awful fake to Rosalinda, but she was here, so she might as well see what they did. Angela opened the door and Rosalinda stepped inside to see a room full of computers. She recognized two women from the streets working on the computers. Ellen saw them and came out of her office. She too walked up to Angela. Ellen said, "Introduce me to your friend."

Angela introduced Rosie and two hours later, Rosalinda was officially a student at Innovation Station. She would start classes the next day. Little did she know how much that day would change her life.

Angela picked up Rosalinda to drive her to the first day of class. Ellen came out and greeted them and immediately escorted Rosalinda to a computer. Rosalinda expected Angela to drop her off, but instead of leaving, she walked into an office in the back. A few minutes later, Angela came back out and began talking with one of the other women working at a computer. She went from computer to computer, checking on each woman. Finally, she walked to Rosalinda's station with a packet in her hand.

"This first class is called Open Door. Here are the instructions and assignments for you to work on," Angela explained.

"What? Wait? You work here?" Rosalinda asked.

"Yes. I make my tacos early in the morning and as soon as I sell out, I come here and work the rest of the day," Angela said.

She went on to explain that she started as a student at Innovation Station and worked her way up to becoming an employee. The Station paid well, but she wanted extra spending money, so she decided to take the classes to open her side business. She loved her job at Innovation Station, she loved making tacos, and she loved the extra money. She also told Rosie some days she had to pinch herself that this was her life. Plus, she was seven months sober.

Rosalinda wanted that life so badly she could taste it.

IMMEDIATE LEADERSHIP OPPORTUNITIES

Rosalinda and Angela's stories intersect to show the power of immediate leadership opportunities. This second principle can be adopted in business or nonprofits organizations supporting survivors to accelerate their development.

What Are Immediate Leadership Opportunities?

Immediate leadership opportunities rely on an advancement structure. Much like a clear promotion path in a company or firm, immediate leadership opportunities rely on a clear path for advancement. At each step along the way, additional responsibilities are assumed by the woman accepting a leadership opportunity. For example, in the program Cheryl developed, the first course that women can take is called Opportunity Knocks, which is a two-week basic computer course. When they complete Opportunity Knocks, they move on to the Acceleration Program. Participants in the Acceleration Program manage the students in Opportunity Knocks. After completing Acceleration, the students can apply for an internship. Interns manage the students in Acceleration. This approach allows women to begin learning leadership skills within the first few weeks of starting the program.

One of the participants in Shannon's study said about immediate leadership opportunities in the program:

> So, we immediately jump in this role. It's not like you don't know what's happening. We all know we don't know what we're doing, but we're going to figure it out as we come along. And then as you look back you are going to say, wow, I did that. I did that. I didn't go to college for it. I wasn't taught, but I was thrown in the role and I figured it out.

There is intentional overlap between immediate leadership opportunities and experiential learning—the first principle. Immediately gaining experiences as a leader that escalate over time provides excellent opportunities for experiential learning. You can see that in the participant's quote. She was talking about the immediate leadership opportunity principle specifically, but her quote showed the interrelationship of experiential learning with phrases like "figure it out."

Survivor Leadership.   An important component of immediate leadership opportunities are the survivor leaders. The term *survivor leader* was used by one of the participants in Shannon's study.[1] The participant used the term to describe survivors of the sex trade (or addiction, domestic violence, etc.) who hold small or large leadership positions in an organization (i.e., teaching a training course, working as the executive director, or serving on the board). Shannon found survivor leadership was critical for several reasons: it gave women hope, it established relatability (and even credibility) through a shared experience, and it modeled a different future through step-ahead mentorship.

First, having survivor leaders—survivors like Angela who were further along in their recovery than survivors like Rosalinda—gave the newer survivor hope. You see it in this story, when Angela models a different future for Rosalinda. One of the participants in Shannon's study, who became a survivor leader, emphasized the importance of survivors who were further along in their recovery providing her hope.

The participant talked about a time she was sitting across from her counselor who was a survivor leader. She described how she "had tattered jeans and a way too short shirt and was still acting a fool 5 months out" and how her counselor/survivor leader "was in a business suit."[2] The participant described how at the time, the counselor said, "You can be where I am. You don't have to ever do this again, and I was where you were 15 years ago and I had no hope."[3] The participant credited survivor leadership with her success and survival. She said, without it "I don't think that I would be here."[4] Seeing her counselor succeed gave the participant hope she could do the same.

Second, survivor leaders are seen as being more relatable than people who had never experienced the sex trade, addiction, poverty, or domestic abuse. When talking about why survivor engagement is important, one of the participants referred to being a survivor as having a "credential"[5] because someone who was not a survivor was not as qualified to support her in her recovery. She said:

> Somebody that has been there done that. You know, because when you're living, when you've lived that kind of lifestyle. You're really, it means a lot to have that, *credential* [emphasis added], or really understand, you know.

Another participant, who had also become a survivor leader, talked about how important it was that women earlier in their journey find mentors who are relatable. As a survivor leader, she said,

> I can relate. Her experiences don't freak me out. . . . No, I can understand. I've been there. I've done that. That's nothing. . . . So, I can break that uniqueness, so that way she can see not our differences, but to see our similarities and that's a good bridge to build.[6]

In contrast, many of the participants in the study talked about how uncomfortable they felt when the "church ladies" or "do-gooders"[7] were the only ones supporting them in their recovery.

We see do-gooders working at the food pantry in Rosalinda's story. Some survivors felt guilt when they compared their lives to those of the church ladies. Further, the women in the study felt they could not be as genuine with the church ladies as they could with other survivors. As one participant, another woman who became a survivor leader, said about the women new to recovery:

> They complain so much about these church women that come in and visit them. "Oh God, here comes the church ladies again." I mean they hate it. They absolutely hate it. And I felt the same way. I felt the same way, because I can't relate to them. What do they know about me? But also, I felt dirty. . . . These women [survivors] when they are in those positions with these [church ladies] they don't have any opportunity to be free, to be themselves, so they're still putting on that mask to deal with these people that are helping them, but they are not being authentic. They have a mask on. Anytime I say this [cuss] she says, "No ma'am don't talk like that," and they call them out on it. . . . They need a chance to be themselves, because they don't get that. They're there all day—case managers, Christian ladies. They [survivors] don't have any opportunity to really let loose and vent. Let it out and be real.

The women in the study felt it was easy to put on a show for the church ladies, but they knew they couldn't get away with that with other survivors. They also didn't need to; they knew they could be themselves and be understood.

Finally, survivor leaders are important because they are step-ahead mentors.[8] A step-ahead mentor, like in the survivor leadership model, has slightly more experience than a peer mentor and less experience than many traditional mentors.[9] Step-ahead mentorship is a well-researched tool for facilitating transformative education, which we have found impactful for women overcoming incarceration, poverty, addiction, or exiting the sex trade. Immediate leadership opportunities harness the power of these survivors or step-ahead mentors. The principle combines hope and relatability. It provides an attainable goal right in front of the survivor—someone like them, who has "been there done that" and now is setting a new goal toward which they can strive.

The Standing Against Global Exploitation (SAGE) Project provides another example of an organization that utilizes immediate leadership opportunities and survivor leadership. They call survivor leaders *peer leaders*, *counselors*, or *educators*. As a nonprofit organization, SAGE supports women who experience drug addiction, sexual exploitation, mental health challenges, and trauma.[10] Hotaling, the founder of SAGE, and colleagues provide another example and insights into the power of the principle we cover in this chapter. About immediate leadership opportunities and survivor leaders providing hope, Hotaling et al., said,

> SAGE counselors serve as role models for clients. Many women who come to SAGE have never made money other than through prostitution. When clients see that others just like themselves have achieved the goals of living independently and outside of the sex industry, they begin to believe they, too, can accomplish this.[11]

SAGE also provides insights into the importance of relatability:

> The experiences of staff allow them to relate sensitively and compassionately to the client's experience of exchanging sex acts for as little as $5, the inability to think of oneself as human but instead a collection of mechanical parts, the compartmentalization of experiences and body parts and the complex dynamics of the pimp/madam-prostitute relationship.

This relatability is in direct contrast to the issue Shannon's participants experience with nonsurvivor volunteers: guilt, shame, and inauthenticity or being able to get something by them. Hotaling et al. said:

> Because of the shame and social stigma associated with prostitution, survivors and those involved feel a greater trust for those who have had similar experiences. "You don't understand" disconnects survivor from the non-survivor (or "straight") counselor. Staff who have lived through recruitment into prostitution and later identified their recruiters/pimps as such will more quickly recognize the same behavior patterns in a client.[12]

Other stories in this book provide examples of survivor leadership that we witnessed. For example, women training each other, helping each other write business plans, and hiring each other. One participant in Shannon's study, who had started a business and provided leadership to many survivors said, "You know they used to have this lifestyle and so you'll know the hiccups that they go through, the self-doubts mainly in our own heads."

In a nonprofit organization supporting women, immediate leadership opportunities through survivor leadership can be modeled after Innovation Station. In a business, immediate leadership opportunities can be achieved through leadership development programs. Even if programs for women overcomers start small, the important component is the opportunity for growth, a clear path forward, and the key requirements described in the next section.

Requirements for Immediate Leadership Opportunities

For this principle—immediate leadership opportunity—to be effective, organizations must adopt an asset-based view of the women they support[13] or employ. An asset-based approach finds its origins in community development. An asset-based approach acknowledges that everyone has talents, gifts, skills, and value. For many organizations working with survivors, the default approach is a needs-based or deficit-based view. A needs- or deficit-based view focuses on what is missing or what isn't working.

A far better approach focuses on what is working and an individual's current strengths, gifts, or skills. Women overcomers cannot be viewed by their deficits; they must be recognized for their strengths. In this book, we present six women with incredible skills, abilities, attributes, and characteristics. They represent phenomenal women, and someone saw that; someone saw them as survivors with great strengths, rather than as victims or even failures.

Some scholars have called for a shift in mental health interventions from a deficit-based view to a strengths-based view.[14] Regarding a deficit-based view to mental health challenges, in particular, O'Hagan said, it "perpetuates inequality and disempowerment, despite its benign intent."[15] The same is true for women overcomers. Too often we have seen well-intentioned organizations treat women as children who could not possibly know what is best for themselves.

A deficit-based view toward women overcoming great challenges fails to position survivors as experts of their own recovery or as mentors for their peers. A deficit-based view makes it easy to focus on failures and to establish rules to prevent failure, rather than to focus on strengths that will give a woman the tools they need to avoid failures on their own and to learn from them when they do occur. An example of an asset-based method for treating survivors of trauma, specifically, is trauma-informed care. Specifically, trauma-informed care works to empower survivors by involving them in making decisions about the services they receive and focuses on survivors' resilience without revictimizing or retraumatizing the survivor.[16]

Once an asset-based view is adopted, it is much easier to position an overcomer as an expert, which is the second requirement of immediate leadership opportunities. The "credentials" survivors gain from making it through tough experiences alone deserves respect. Hotaling et al. said, "survival is a testament to one's capabilities."[17] Though she was talking specifically about survivors of the sex trade, the same holds true in other contexts. The accomplishment of surviving incarceration, poverty, addiction, sex trade, domestic violence, and so on deserves acknowledgment. Survivors are experts in their own experience, in survival, and in what women with similar experiences need to move forward.

Regardless of an employee's background, we have a tendency as businesses to focus more on weaknesses than strengths. Implementing immediate leadership opportunities requires companies to replace a deficit-based view with an asset-based view. Such a perspective change may require a cultural shift within the organization. Now is a great time for such a shift. Positive organizational development approaches in business shift leaders' focus from solving problems by addressing organizations' (or individual's) weaknesses to focusing on using their strengths to improve outcomes. Such an approach includes appreciative inquiry (AI). AI focuses on what an organization does well, rather than what it needs to improve.[18] By focusing on the organizations' strengths, the organization can co-construct an improved future by maximizing on what the organization does when it is at its best. AI is the organization-wide version of a strength-based approach for individuals.

The SOAR analysis is another positively oriented strategic planning tool. SOAR stands for strengths, opportunities, aspirations, and results. The model replaces the well-known SWOT analysis, which stands for strengths, weaknesses, opportunities, and threats. As you can see from the components of SOAR, the focus is on strengths and not the deficits of the organization or individual.

Even in performance evaluations, we often focus on employee's weaknesses or areas for improvement. However, it is critical to focus on strengths, which can be done through professional development assessments such as CliftonStrengths. CliftonStrengths focuses on an individual's top five strengths. Their philosophy is that an individual can much more effectively magnify their strengths to improve their leadership abilities, rather than trying to improve weaker areas.

Shannon experienced a significant shift in her leadership style when she started asking her team, "What processes need to change to help us improve?" It was a question they asked in weekly meetings. Rather than focusing on any employee's weaknesses or deficits, the team focused on creating processes to mitigate the impact of any weaknesses and maximize strengths.

The shift can be challenging and met with skepticism. However, it has worked for many organizations that have embraced a positive organizational approach to improve everything from customer service to supply chain efficiency. Companies such as Apple, Johnson & Johnson, and The Coca-Cola Company have used AI for these purposes.[19]

If you are reading this book because you are hoping to find cheap labor, read a different book. The goal is not to find women who can be underpaid, but to find women who have a unique skill set and can add incredible value to an organization.

Unfortunately, even when survivors are viewed from an asset-based approach and their expertise is acknowledged, their pay often does not reflect such knowledge. An additional requirement of immediate leadership opportunities is that survivors' pay be appropriate for the position, with the goal of paying a livable wage as early in a promotion track as possible. Certainly, this is the case in businesses hiring survivors and even for nonprofits developing a program with survivor leadership. We have seen and heard from too many women overcomers who are not making a living wage for work they do or for the expertise they provide. If you are reading this book because you are hoping to find cheap labor, read a different book. The goal is not to find women who can be underpaid, but to find women who have a unique skill set and can add incredible value to an organization. It is critical to pay a fair wage for the expertise and unique perspective they bring. If you don't, they will take their talents elsewhere, and the organization will never capitalize on these overcomers living and working to their full potential.

Finally, and related to the issue of fair pay, is the need to take care to not revictimize survivors. Underpaying is a way corporations and organizations risk revictimizing survivors, but revictimization plays into other aspects of working with women who have experienced trauma. You saw in Cara's story, the crude jokes were a form of re-traumatizing a survivor. One way to mitigate the risk of revictimization for all employees within your organization is to engage survivors. They are well-equipped to guide policy that will reduce the risk of victimization or revictimization.

Creating Immediate Leadership Opportunities

Whether your organization is a corporation considering hiring survivors or a nonprofit organization supporting them, there is a great deal to learn from the immediate leadership opportunity model. The following questions can help your organization identify areas where you might be ready to use an immediate leadership model.

- Do we have areas in our business with clear opportunities for career progression?
- Do any of the career paths allow employees to start without specified experience or expertise?
- In what areas could we give employees more power over their work environment by positioning them as experts in creating a favorable workplace?
- In what areas could we give employees more power over their career progression to position them as experts in their own lives?

- Do we have policies and practices in place to ensure pay is fair and equitable but also sustainable for our employees?
- Are there areas where our culture needs to improve to ensure survivors of any trauma are not revictimized?
- In what ways do we view employees from a deficit-based focus?
- Are managers in our organization prepared to support employees who have experienced trauma?

Organizations ready to implement immediate leadership opportunity have an amazing opportunity to accelerate women's transition from challenging pasts, like Rosalinda.

DARING TO DREAM

Yes, Rosalinda wanted the life Angela was experiencing. But her biggest fear was that this life didn't want her. She didn't tell George she signed up at the Innovation Station. She was positive he would explode if he found out. He liked the fact that she was dependent on him. He didn't want her moving on. She was his pet who he could do whatever he wanted with.

As if Angela was reading her thoughts, she said, "When are you going to get away from George? We both know he is bad for you."

Rosalinda dropped her eyes and said, "I can't. I love him."

"Well, you may love him, but he sure as hell doesn't love you. And you know it." Angela shot back.

Rosalinda knew it was true. George brought other women over all the time. She would have to sleep on the couch those nights. The truth was she feared George more than she loved him. She feared life without George more than she loved him. She had nowhere to go. She had no job, no money, nothing. That was the sick part of her life: she was stuck.

As soon as Rosalinda thought she was stuck, the computer on the desk in front of her caught her attention. She was in a program. She was learning new skills. She was here because she was willing to try to do something different. It was the first time she realized she didn't *need* George. She could make it on her own. She survived on the streets on her own every time George went to jail. Hell, most of the time she did better than just survive. She may not have had a place to live all the time, but she took care of business. But if she wanted to keep coming here, she had to have a place to stay. She doubted they would let a stinky homeless person take these classes.

Again, as if Angela knew what she was thinking she said, "Why don't you go to Community Builders? I heard they provide rental assistance to people trying to make changes."

Rosalinda quickly frowned. She was not going to Community Builders. She heard about it from other women who went there and left right away. They all said the same thing, "Community Builders had too many rules."

Angela, shot back, "Yeah. Rules are much worse than life with George!" as she turned and walked away.

Angela picked Rosalinda up every day that week after she sold all her tacos. One day Rosalinda asked about Community Builders. Angela told her to talk to the other ladies at the Innovation Station because most of them were in Community Builders' program. And so, she did. Each one of them said the same thing. Yes, there were rules, but it was a good deal. They were safe and had their own small efficiency units and were excited to start a new life. They had a case-worker that came by frequently to check to make sure there were no extra residents or "chemicals" around. But most of the caseworkers were great and really supported the residents.

At the end of the day, on the way home, Angela told Rosalinda if she ever decided she wanted to go to Community Builders, to let her know. All she had to do was pick a day George would be gone. Angela told her she would help her pack and take her there. Two days later, the back seat of Angela's car was loaded down with trash bags of clothes, shoes, and all Rosalinda's personal treasures.

Going to Community Builders was the best thing Rosalinda did. The other women were right. She had her own place. Rosalinda made her bed and looked around the room before she left for the Innovation Station. It was a small room. A brown dresser that had seen a few too many moves sat in the corner. The pink pillowcase draped over the top covered most of the deep scratches. On top were several pictures of her mom and some of her personal items. She had a small table next to her bed with her favorite glass bluebird of happiness sitting next to the bowl that held her jewelry. The white plastic laundry basket on the floor next to the closet took up most of the only open floor space. Her favorite part of the room was her bed, where her ratty blue stuffed dog sat limply on her pillow. Even though she was a grown woman, when she got to pick out the comforter for her bed, she chose a Strawberry Shortcake quilt.

Rosalinda's cousin Jessica had Strawberry Shortcake sheets when they were little. The last time Rosalinda felt safe was sleeping at Jessica's house in those sheets. Rosalinda's mother dropped her off for the weekend one day and never came back. Her aunt loved her but was not in a place to take her in, so Rosalinda was placed in foster care until one thing led to another and she was living with George.

Shaking off the thoughts of George, she focused on the fact that she had her own place. And her caseworker was the best. One of the perks of being in the program was the opportunity to work at several local companies part-time while they were in transition. Rosalinda was hired at Capital Equipment and Supplies. The first day on the job her boss told her she would be working in stocking. She also went on to say they were always looking to promote people who work hard and bring innovation to the business. She told her about the promotion program and introduced her to her mentor who was one step ahead of her at Capital. Rosalinda knew she was a hard worker, and sure enough, three months after being hired, she was promoted to supervisor of all the stockers.

Some days Rosalinda had to pinch herself thinking about all the amazing things that she was experiencing. She was working and getting an opportunity to lead at her job. She was learning from great leaders at the Station. Her future seemed to be limitless. Rosalinda looked at the clock and realized she needed to get going and headed off to the Innovation Station.

When she finished the curriculum for the first class—Open Door— she signed up for classes in the Freedom Capital Ventures (FCV) program. FCV was a course about starting a business that went from the basics all the way to creating a business plan. While she was in the FCV courses, she was required to help students that signed up for the Open Door classes that she had just completed. Helping and managing the students was eye-opening for Rosalinda. She began to appreciate both her former teachers and employers.

Like Angela, she wanted to open her own business, so she worked hard in the FCV courses, which Angela had helped develop. Angela mentored Rosalinda in developing a business plan to launch Mariposa Pastries. She loved baking and with this new venture, she could make extra money on the side while she worked at Capital. Her plan was to bake and deliver pastries in the morning before work. She would bake whatever orders she received each day in the evening and deliver them on the way to work the next day. To start, she took the small amount of money she saved and designed and printed some flyers and ordered business cards.

When Rosalinda got her business cards, she squealed like a kid. She rushed to show then to Angela. She was officially in business. Both of them were just as giddy laughing until Rosalinda lost it. She fell apart. Slumping over the table, she let loose and sobbed.

Angela walked over, sat beside her, laid her hand on her back, and said, "Let it out. I understand."

Rosalinda knew she did. It was only eleven months earlier Angela launched Uno, Dos, Tacos. So, Rosalinda took her advice and cried until she had no more tears to cry.

WHY IMMEDIATE LEADERSHIP OPPORTUNITIES WORK

Implementing immediate leadership opportunities works because it allows women overcomers to immediately start practicing their workplace skills. Using survivor leaders, or step-ahead mentors, provides hope and a model of what it looks like to move forward in lawful employment.

One primary benefit of immediate leadership opportunities is the pride overcomers experience through legitimate employment. In

Shannon's study, the participants found a great deal of self-worth from working—both from making money and from being productive. As one participant said,

> You start to build self-worth and self-esteem, because you have a job and you're doing something. . . . Having a purpose, feeling needed, feeling like I was doing something productive, like I was a productive member of society . . . and not feeling like I was on the opposite side. Starting to feel like I was on the right side, I think really helped . . . integrate me into society.

Embracing immediate leadership opportunities allowed women overcomers to experience success and independence, while giving them hope for the future.

As other participants said, it was often some of the small things that gave them hope—being able to pay for a place to live, having cable, or owning a car. One participant said,

> You know, so I never would have imagined I had all of my own stuff and my own house, and doing it all on my own. . . . I feel like I could do anything. . . . You know, my life is just so much different. It's just great. I mean, I own a home. . . . I know material things don't matter, but in a sense to me, having a house, and a working vehicle and food in the pantry and my bills paid, like that is a big defining factor of my life, you know. That does show my value. I mean, we love our home, we respect it and we take care of it.

For her and many others, the ability to make money shifted their self-worth from being dependent on the way they were viewed by men, like George, to being independent and based on their own accomplishments. Immediate leadership is powerful.

If you are a nonprofit organization supporting women overcomers, immediate leadership opportunity is the only way we have seen economic empowerment work. We have seen traditional job-training programs work but never as well as an organization using immediate leadership opportunities as a training ground for overcomers. Immediate leadership opportunities provide survivors a safe place to learn and grow. These immediate leadership opportunities, unlike more traditional training programs, provide real work with real consequences, real rewards, and real opportunities to lead.

We talk to many organizations who say they don't have the resources to start a social enterprise. If you have participants, then you have resources. Programs that effectively implement immediate leadership opportunities do not require as many outside resources. Such programs can fund themselves. You don't need personnel or a building to get started. You need overcomers, who are looking to gain experiences that will help them in the workplace. Let the women overcomers research the unmet need in your community and start a business to address it. Then make sure those survivors and the ones who come after them make a living wage as soon as possible. Honestly, the model is not hard to implement. The hardest part for most people to overcome is a deficit-based mindset. Once they do, they can harness the power of immediate leadership opportunities. Are you going to hold on to the deficit-based mindset or are you going to trust in a strength- and asset-based model?

MAKING IT HAPPEN

The phone buzzed in Rosalinda's pocket. Without a thought she snatched it to her ear and answered quickly. She never wanted to take a chance of missing a potential job. But the voice on the line was one she immediately recognized, and it was not about business.

"Mom? Is that you?" Carrie asked timidly.

Rosalinda froze. She knew she needed to respond, but no words escaped her lips.

"Hello . . . Mom?" Carrie repeated.

Rosalinda forced herself to speak, "Carrie, baby, oh baby, it is so good to hear your voice."

Carrie explained that she saw the advertisements for Mariposa Pastries. She went on to say, that for years she hated Rosalinda for choosing George over her and her brothers. Carrie shared she had been watching Rosie from a distance to make sure she was really changed. Carrie kept in touch with several people from Rosalinda's past, and they all reassured her Rosie was a different person. And now, as a mom herself, she knew she needed to forgive, especially because George was no longer in the picture.

Again, Rosalinda couldn't speak. All she could do was cry. She had longed and waited for this moment for years, but she also knew it would have to be when Carrie was ready. She was thrilled that day finally came; they made plans to meet the following day at the park.

Rosalinda could not believe her eyes when she saw Carrie sitting under the tree at Hopkins Park. Her long brown hair braided in pigtails made her look childlike but her beautiful face was that of a grown woman. Looking up, Carrie saw her mom approach. They stood two feet apart, staring with nervous anticipation until Carrie opened her arms, and they fell together in an embrace that was ten years in the making. The rest of the afternoon, they talked and laughed. Rosalinda had never met her two grandchildren, and they were as beautiful as their mother. Lily was four with long brown hair like her mother. Carlos was three and so full of energy he never stopped. That afternoon was glorious and the start of a new season for Rosalinda. There would be many more afternoons and evenings with mother and daughter reconnecting.

Rosalinda knew she was good at her job at Capital. And just as expected, Mariposa Pastries began to grow. Rosalinda needed help. She loved her job at Capital, and she loved Mariposa. She didn't want to choose between them, so she decided to hire someone to help with her business. She reached out to the Innovation Station and hired Margaret, a recent graduate from their internship program. She not only trained Margaret, but she also mentored her. She helped her understand how relationships and communication affected business as well as regular life. Just as she was mentoring Margaret, she was being mentored at Capital. This was the main reason she loved her job. Her hard work and effective management of the stockers caught the eye of Harrison, the manager of one of Capital's leading product lines. Harrison approached Rosalinda and asked if she would be interested in the Capital's program that trained potential employees to become lead managers in different areas. Of course, Rosalinda wanted to advance her career and seized the opportunity.

A year later, Rosie was managing employees at Capital, and Margaret was doing so well with Mariposa that Rosie had to hire an additional employee, Annie, who also came from the Innovation Station. Margaret trained and mentored Annie the same way she had been trained. Rosie still helped with baking, but for the most part, Margaret ran the business. Rosalinda knew how valuable Margaret was to Mariposa, so she made sure she earned the money she deserved—enough to comfortably support herself and her children.

Having trusted hardworking employees allowed Rosalinda to focus on her job at Capital. She was making good money now and didn't need her side business. But she loved baking. She also loved that she was providing jobs to women who had been just like her. Her product line at Capital was one of the most efficient in the company. Her leadership approach with her employees was exactly how she was taught by her supervisors at Capital and the leaders at Innovation Station. She provided employees autonomy and opportunities to lead. Once in leadership, employees took their responsibilities on the job far more seriously. They worked harder and developed new ideas to increase efficiency and productivity. When employees developed viable ideas, their leadership opportunities were expanded in meaningful ways.

Rosalinda didn't always have the authority to reward this leadership or innovation with a pay increase, so she found other ways to compensate good leadership and innovation. She provided opportunities for flex time so employees could do simple things like attend school events of their children or counseling appointments for themselves. She also rewarded good leadership with opportunities for employees to participate in activities at work they enjoyed. One woman on her team loved

> Like you can't un-ring a bell, you cannot unknow the discovery of untapped, unlimited potential.

softball, so when Rosalinda saw her effective leadership on the team, she asked her if she would be interested in organizing an employee intramural league. The woman was delighted, and before she knew it, half of the crew joined a team. Rosalinda also coordinated monthly celebrations of accomplishments and new ideas and she brought Mariposa pastries. Her employees were incredible. Like her, once they realized their leadership potential, they were hooked. Like you can't un-ring a bell, you cannot unknow the discovery of untapped, unlimited potential.

The increased efficiency of Rosalinda's department did not go unnoticed. Todd Matthews, the COO of Capital, called her into his office. He began by acknowledging the incredible performance level her department maintained, excelling in every key performance indicator. And not only were they productive, but her employee turnover was also almost nonexistent, which was rare for their type of jobs.

He looked at her skeptically and asked, "Do you know why your unit is so effective or is it a fluke?"

A *fluke?* She took a deep breath to shake the frustration and said, "Of course I know. ROAR."

"What?" Todd asked, more confused than impressed.

"ROAR is our motto—rewards, opportunities, autonomy, and relate. It's my leadership philosophy. And my team loves it."

Rosalinda continued. "Rewards are motivators, so I implemented a reward system, but the best rewards are important to the employee on the inside. I explained to my team that I expected each of them to be leaders and if they led well, they would be rewarded."

That caught Todd off guard. Rosalinda explained that some of her team members had experienced challenges in life, and they needed to know what success felt like.

Rosie continued, "Then I give everyone opportunities. When someone rises to the occasion of the opportunity, they get more autonomy. Finally, I work to relate to everyone. That doesn't mean being friends with everyone. It just means trying to understand what is important to them."

She explained she provided raises to her top performers based on the company's annual merit review policies, but that meant she couldn't always reward good work monetarily. So, knowing what was important to her employees allowed her to get creative in giving them rewards.

"Whose philosophy is that? I didn't learn it in B school," Todd asked.

Head slightly tilted, Rosalinda said. "I'm not sure what B school means. I just developed the ROAR acronym so we could all be on the same page."

Todd was impressed and asked if ROAR was a concept that could be implemented company-wide and Rosalinda quickly said it could.

That meeting led to several other meetings, and three months later, Todd created a new position for Rosalinda as a training director. Her role would focus on training managers in ROAR. Rosalinda was shocked when she got the compensation package for her new role. Her salary was more than double what it had been before. Not only was she to oversee managers in this branch of Capital, but she was also to do so in all the other branches as well. And like everything Rosalinda tackled, she excelled.

She loved her job and she loved seeing people begin to love working for Capital instead of dreading going to work. Of course, there were days that made her want to scream. Like the time she went for her first meeting with managers in the distribution center in Dallas. She was in the conference room preparing when the last of the local managers walked in.

When he saw Rosalinda, he said, "Hey, when you finish here can you check on the men's room. We are out of paper towels and someone left the sink running, so water is all over the floor that needs to be mopped up."

Rosalinda's cheeks flashed bright read. *He thinks I am in custodial services. Is it because I am Latina, a woman, the way I am dressed, or all of the above?* The comment rattled her confidence briefly.

"I'm sorry. I'm about to begin this meeting. Can you please see if custodial services can address the issues in the men's room?" *I am sorry? Ugh, why are women always apologizing.* That was a fight for another day. She needed to compose herself, so with that she walked to the front of the room to begin the meeting. The most disgusting part of that encounter was the man who made the comment only shrugged and sat down. He was not embarrassed or apologetic in any way. Rosalinda proceeded with the meeting.

But even with incidents like that, Rosalinda's life was perfect. She was successful by every standard. She was a leader. She was also a mom that was headed over to Carrie's for dinner for their weekly get together. As usual, when she arrived, the two embraced. Carrie had prepared her mom's favorite meal. Afterward, Rosalinda spent the evening playing with Lily and Carlos. She was about to leave when Lily begged her to tuck her into bed. Rosalinda glanced at Carrie, who nodded. Lily crawled into her bed and Rosalinda sat beside her. She could not believe this was happening. It was as if she was looking down on the same bed so many years ago staring into the eyes of her sweet Carrie. But this was Lily and the love Rosalinda had for this baby girl was overwhelming.

A tear dropped from her eye as she whispered, "I love you forever. Forever and always. To the moon and back my sweet baby girl."

HERE'S THE CHECK

Entrepreneurial Culture

"Congratulations, here's the check," said Roseanne, the loan officer at the local bank.

Emmie froze and stood there looking at the envelope being handed to her. *Wow, is this real? Is this really happening?* Emmie couldn't believe it was only five months ago she stumbled through the doors of the Hope House. She remembered that time so well. Well, not the first few days, but every day after.

Numbness oozed through Emmie's limbs as she shuffled down the street. Her brain was as tousled as her matted hair, but she was oblivious to both. All she could feel in the moment was exhaustion and not exhaustion that comes from a late night out or working too hard. This exhaustion came from weeks of using crack and endless highs keeping sleep at bay. This exhaustion seeps in deep, making your bones ache. These past nine months were worse than her previous relapses. It was as if the dope was better at slapping her body around but less effective at getting her high.

When she didn't think she could take another step, she saw the blue door to the housing program she had left nine months ago. Her original stay at Hope House was short-lived, but she remembered the kind lady who welcomed her that first time. The fog in her mind kept Emmie from remembering her name, but she could still see the woman's gentle eyes. Those eyes drew Emmie back to the safety of that blue door. So did the truth she held deep inside: if she didn't reach out, she would soon die.

Agnes, the kind lady Emmie couldn't remember, opened the door to see a filthy, frail, shadow of a woman. After escorting her to the intake office, Agnes asked the woman her name.

Crooking her head slightly Emmie said, "It's me. Emmie."

"Oh my, Emmie. I didn't recognize you," responded Agnes with surprise.

Agnes was the program coordinator when Emmie stayed at Hope House the first time. Agnes knew and loved Emmie well, but this woman in front of her was hardly Emmie.

Emmie was too tired to be embarrassed. All she knew is that she wanted to sleep somewhere safe, and if that meant dealing with the wide-eyed drop-jawed reaction of Agnes, she would deal with it. Agnes composed herself, returning back to her gentle expression and began asking questions. Most of the questions were about what would be different if they allowed her to come back. Emmie didn't hear the words coming out of her mouth, but whatever she said must have worked because the next thing Emmie knew she was being led to the cozy room in the back corner of the second floor. Agnes didn't even make Emmie face Carol, the Hope House director, who could see right through any excuses Emmie might have tried to use. And two hours later after a long shower and a hot meal, she was tucked into the soft covers under a tattered comforter drifting off to deep sleep.

Emmie knew the routine. She cherished those first two weeks, where, like a baby, all she did was eat and sleep. It was time to let her mind settle—a time mixed with staring off the porch, mindlessly rocking on the white wooden chair. She wore a shirt with a Pomeranian on the front that Agnes had grabbed from the bin. She imagined the undoubtably sweet, and surely old, woman who dropped it off after cleaning out her closet.

After those first few weeks, two exciting things happened. First, while Emmie had been on the streets her aunt had been raising Emmie's children, but her aunt saw Emmie's determination and agreed that it would be best for the children to live with Emmie at Hope House; after all, she was their mother. Second, Emmie also started taking classes at the Dream Center—the social enterprise run by the women at the Hope House. It was the second day at the center that Emmie knew this was going to be good, and she was determined to learn all she could. She was learning so much from the courses, but she was learning even more from the mentors at the Dream Center. They were women just like her—overcomers—and they formed a great support system with an entrepreneurial focus. For the last month, Emmie had worked on a business plan with her mentor, Jessica. Jessica launched her own business the prior year and was the first woman at the Dream Center to receive a microloan. She used it to open Jess's Messes, a sloppy sandwich food truck. The sandwich business was only open Monday through Thursday. Jessica would love to be open seven days a week, but cash flow kept her to just four days for now. Her goal was to build slowly to ensure long-term stability. In the meantime, Jessica also worked at the Dream Center on Fridays helping women like she was helped. Emmie knew Jess from the streets. They sat in many dope houses together before Jess decided to leave and try for a sober life. When Emmie saw all that Jess was able to accomplish in just one year, she decided to give it a try as well. And here she was, following in Jessica's footsteps.

Four months from when she walked into the door of Hope House, Emmie was wide awake and ready to go as she sat in the office of First Union Bank waiting for the Leadership Resource Team (LRT). She was about to pitch her idea for a new business to this "shark tank."

Emmie had a hard time not seeing the business leaders as sharks, even though Carol explained, "The LRT is on your side. They aren't sharks out to get you."

As the director of Hope House, Carol had been on Emmie's side for many years, even if Carol did constantly push Emmie to be better and not let her get away with any BS. Even if she found it hard to believe the sharks weren't out to get her, Emmie could imagine the sharks as playing the same role as Carol—supportive but tough.

Emmie also understood her idea needed to be vetted before she stood any chance of getting approved for the small loan. Emmie shuffled through the papers in front of her for the hundredth time that morning. She was about to meet with bankers and lawyers and really smart businesspeople. *What if they hated her idea? Why in the world did she think she was smart enough to open a coffee shop? What was she thinking when she came up with the name Coffee and Bananas?* It sounded so stupid rolling around in her mind now. Just when she got worked up enough to bolt from the room, the door opened to laughter and conversations. It was too late; the team was here. She would have to present her plan. Over the next hour, Emmie explained her idea of combining coffee with creative arts. Her target market was young mothers. Her unique business combined good coffee and creative art projects moms could buy and do with their children as they enjoyed coffee with other moms and their children. She was shocked when the team said they loved the idea. They also said they were concerned about her break-even point and margins. They told her to look into those details, as well as the unit costs. After scheduling a follow-up meeting for a month later, they all got up to leave. After the team was gone, Emmie allowed herself to jump up and squeal. Carol just smiled and helped her pack up the coffee samples and art projects she brought to show the team.

Emmie returned to the Dream Center. She had some work to do. Every day for the next three weeks, Emmie researched, adjusted numbers, and looked for lowest prices for initial capital expenditures to start Coffee and Bananas and for the inventory to keep it going. She was extremely proud of the hard work she put in to make her dream a reality. The most exciting part of her business plan was the location of her shop.

Carter's Plumbing was a large company in the community. The main space was open to the public for general plumbing needs, including a kitchen and bath showcase. There was an old apartment above the main building. Outside the door of the apartment was a larger rooftop space that covered the massive storage section of Carter's.

Carter's was down the street from Hope House and did the plumbing at the house for years. More importantly, Carter's had partnered with the home. Their primary focus was to hire women seeking employment in sales. But the last few years they were heavily invested in the work at the Dream Center. They provided mentors for women seeking to create a business or for those pursuing employment.

Carter's increased their commitment this year by entering into an agreement with the Center to create a business incubator.

Emmie was approved to be the first business to incubate in the space above Carter's. There were so many wins in this situation. Coffee and Bananas would pay minimal rent for the space, keeping overhead down. Employees at Carter's would have access to great coffee and breakfast treats. Several employees with young families expressed interest in purchasing Emmie's art projects to use on the weekends with their children. And the owners of Carter's were making a profit by renting the unused space, while also making a difference.

The day before the second meeting with the LRT, Jessica and Emmie reviewed the final changes to the business plan. Emmie had worked hard, and it showed.

Jessica looked at the professional cover and said, "You have really done a great job, Em. I am so proud of you. And almost a little jealous."

Hearing those words from Jessica, Emmie started to cry. No one had ever been proud of her before. But she realized she should be proud. For the past five months, she had busted her butt to develop this idea. And it was also during those same five months she was doing the agonizing work of recovery from fifteen years of addiction to crack and alcohol. Wow, she was sober and hopefully about to launch her business.

The morning of the meeting, Emmie had several flavors of hot coffee and mixings on the table ready for the LRT. She also brought a batch of her favorite maple banana walnut muffins. Everyone who tried her muffins raved over them, and she couldn't wait for the team to try them. The team arrived and the process began again. They scoured every page of her proposal, pointing out strengths, acknowledging changes, and asking question after question. For a while Emmie thought she might not have done enough. *Why were they asking so many questions? Did they hate her plan?*

Finally, Tom, the chair of the LRT said, "This is a great plan and looks like a sound and profitable business."

Robert, another business owner said, "You have taken a business that typically has small margins and increased them significantly with your concept of art projects. Very impressive."

Tom said, "We like your proposal, but we are recommending a loan amount of $5,000."

Emmie only asked for $3,000 to start Coffee and Bananas, but the team said they felt she really needed *more* to make sure the business had enough backing for a solid start. Emmie just sat there staring. She tried to open her mouth, but it was as if it was glued shut. She wanted to say something, but the words "$5,000" and "recommending" floating around in her brain were just so unexpected she couldn't quite grasp the meaning, much less how to respond.

"Sooooo, are you going to accept the recommendation and $5,000?" Carol asked.

Emmie realized she had been sitting there silent for too long. Red flushed across her cheeks and her forehead glistened as she forced her mouth to open.

Finally, she fumbled out the words, "Uh . . . yeah . . . I mean, yes. Of course, I will."

ENTREPRENEURIAL CULTURE

Emmie's story exemplifies the power of an entrepreneurial culture— the third principle that amplifies businesses' ability to make an impact.

What Is an Entrepreneurial (or Intrapreneurial) Culture in an Organization?

Innovation can be fostered or squashed, depending on how entrepreneurial the culture is in an organization. Entrepreneurial culture involves creating an environment that encourages innovation, creativity, adaptability, and continuous improvement. Organizations that are particularly entrepreneurial provide incentives for innovation and accept failure, which will happen with entrepreneurial endeavors.

Any organization can adopt an entrepreneurial culture—including a nonprofit organization, a small business, a large corporation, or anything in between. We talk about entrepreneurial culture in two main contexts within an organization: within the nonprofit organizations supporting women overcomers and within for-profit organizations from start-ups to well-established corporations. Nonprofits might help women start their own business, in the way that the Dream Center supported Emmie. Adopting an entrepreneurial culture in that context is critically important. We will also spend a significant portion of this chapter talking about how businesses can benefit from hiring women who have overcome challenging pasts by fostering their entrepreneurial spirits.

Although Emmie was working to start a business, a new venture is not a necessary condition when creating an entrepreneurial culture. We have certainly seen an entrepreneurial culture positively impact women and their communities when they are starting their own businesses. But large corporations can also reap significant rewards from adopting this principle. If corporations adopt and encourage innovation, those corporations can then also benefit from employing women overcomers because of their propensity for possessing an entrepreneurial spirit.

In the context of larger corporations, an entrepreneurial culture might be best captured through intrapreneurship. *Intrapreneurship* is a term believed to have been coined by Gifford Pinchot III and Elizabeth S. Pinchot in the late 1970s. Intrapreneurs are entrepreneurial employees within a large corporation. As employees, they "do for corporate innovation what an entrepreneur does for his or her start-up."[1] The Pinchots recognized a problem still facing many large corporations today—turning a large cruise ship is much harder than moving a nimble speed boat. Pointing to large organizations, the Pinchots said what they needed was a more entrepreneurial culture— "something akin to free market entrepreneurship within the corporate organization,"[2] not more regulation.

The Pinchots saw intrapreneurship as a way of "solving the problems of large-scale organizations" through empowered innovation. When the Pinchots first coined the term *intrapreneurs* they presented several principles that they speculated would be useful in fostering creativity and innovations within a corporation. The following principles still provide a valuable roadmap for corporations reading this chapter, who are considering implementing intrapreneurial projects within their organization.

- The intrapreneur should incur some risk, even if it is just the loss of time invested in a project.
- The intrapreneur should be able to request funding for a project by presenting a well-developed proposal.
- The project should involve a shared reward—"well-defined and equitable." This means the company alone cannot benefit from the project. A shared reward could include a bonus or "intracapital." Intracapital is money set aside from the profits of successful projects that the successful intrapreneur can invest in a new project.
- Autonomy should be granted regarding the use of the intracapital. The intrapreneur's successful project should earn them enough trust to be given freedom and flexibility to pursue another project with few limitations and questions from the company.
- Successful intrapreneurs could invest their intracapital in other intrapreneurs' projects, like venture capitalists within the firm.

With the right adjustments and a few small experiments, any business can also implement an entrepreneurial (or intrapreneurial) culture.

For simplicity, going forward, we will use the term *entrepreneurial culture* to capture the spirit of innovation, creativity, adaptability, and continuous improvement in any organization—nonprofit, for-profit, large or small. However, we mean the term to capture *intrapreneurship* as well.

An entrepreneurial culture can be present in any individual or group—organizations, communities, and countries. Some combination of an entrepreneurial environment and certain individual characteristics are necessary to fully capitalize on an entrepreneurial culture. Before we dive into the requirements for creating an entrepreneurial culture, it is important to understand what makes women overcomers particularly equipped with an entrepreneurial spirit.

An Individual's Entrepreneurial Culture or Nature

We have found many women in recovery, formerly incarcerated, from generational poverty, or survivors from the sex trade are intuitively entrepreneurial. They may also be more willing to take risks, which can be a beautiful by-product of their devastating pasts. After experiencing failure, the fear of failure can, at times, lose its power. Cheryl recalled a woman in her program whose coworker's husband had been laid off. The coworker was terribly upset and panicked about losing everything. The woman in Cheryl's program said she would not panic in the same situation. She knew if she lost everything, it would not be the end of the world. She had nothing before and survived, if it happened again, she knew she would survive again. Coming to that realization was freeing in the context of entrepreneurship as well.

The women's entrepreneurial intuition was previously focused in areas not valued by society. Cheryl saw the entrepreneurial spirit in women who rode their bikes ten miles each way to steal and sell jeans. Through our work, we've seen the drug dealers with a work ethic we all wish we could muster. The effort just wasn't directed toward lawful businesses valued by society. We will talk more about this in chapter 4.

Creating an entrepreneurial culture in nonprofit organizations providing support or in small businesses or large corporations providing jobs can unlock potential in women who know what it means to fight against the odds.

Scholars don't know for sure what characteristics or personality traits lead to successful entrepreneurs. However, some studies have found common characteristics of successful entrepreneurs, which include innovation, self-esteem or self-efficacy, and a need for self-achievement.[3] Others have found creative initiative, risk tolerance, autonomy, commitment, and persistence to be important drivers.[4]

Despite the debate, in every study we uncovered, the personality traits outlined were characteristics of women overcomers, like those in in this book, had in spades. Common attributes, skills, or characteristics across participants in Shannon's study included resourcefulness and the ability to "hustle."[5] Perhaps the most important characteristic among women in Shannon's study, which you will see in Emmie's story, is the resilience—the ability to get back up again and again.

Those characteristics served women well on the streets and translated perfectly to entrepreneurship. Regardless of debate and contradictions in scholarly literature about what makes a good entrepreneur, it was obvious that the women's persistence and tenacity in getting back up again and again is what made them successful entrepreneurs.

The getting back up again just needed to happen in an environment of a supportive entrepreneurial culture to tap into the entrepreneurial spirit and motivation within survivors like Emmie and Jessica.

Years ago, Cheryl was having a conversation with a business leader in the community. She was working with him to develop a program much like the LRT partnering with Emmie. The business leader made a comment about how the project was such a challenging endeavor to take on considering the "fragility" of the women Cheryl's organization served. Starting a business is challenging and many new businesses don't stand the test of time. He thought experiencing another failure could have a negative impact on the women. Cheryl's first thought was, *Oh, yeah, they are fragile. . . . I didn't think about that.* Then she quickly thought, *What am I thinking? Our women aren't fragile. They are strong, courageous, tenacious, and resilient.* Cheryl learned from the women time and time again that they were resilient, not fragile. One time, Cheryl was working with a woman who launched her own business several months earlier. The woman hit a significant roadblock and wanted to shut down her business.

Cheryl asked her, "What makes this obstacle big enough to close your business?"

She replied, "I just don't want to fail."

Cheryl, with her perfect combination of care and challenge, said to her with an encouraging laugh, "You have been failing your whole life. You failed at recovery. You failed as a parent. You are an expert at failure. At least this time if you fail it will be doing something productive. And you know, even if you fail the first try, you will recover like you always do."

She laughed and said, "That's not even funny, but it's true."

A month later, the entrepreneur had overcome the challenge and had a successful business. Most likely, some combination of certain individual characteristics and an entrepreneurial environment are necessary for success for those who successfully launch a business.

Requirements for an Entrepreneurial Culture

First, when we talk about requirements for an entrepreneurial culture, these are not *necessarily* the same criteria that would be essential to successfully run your own venture. We are not talking about the requirements for long sleepless nights and business understanding. Here, we are focused on the requirements for creating an entrepreneurial culture in organizations hoping to unlock that spirit in women overcomers.

The elements necessary for the entrepreneurial culture to work well include support, willingness to fail, tolerance of uncertainty, elimination of red tape, ownership, and a well-defined reward system. These elements are based on research about what is required for all organizations, but we provide applications specific to women who have experienced challenging pasts of incarceration, poverty, addiction, or engagement in the sex trade.

Scholars have found support from various sources is a critical element in entrepreneurial success.[6] Sources for support range from the macrolevel, such as support from a country's central government, down to the microlevel, such as support from families. The lesson is important for organizations encouraging overcomers' entrepreneurial efforts. For many of the women, traditional support was broken. They may have experienced incarceration and severed familial ties. Support from a recovery organization may be all they have initially. For many women in Shannon's study, the love they received from the nonprofit organizations supporting them was critical. It filled a gap often left by family and provided unconditional love. As one participant said, "I think they kind of filled that void of what a family is supposed to do. . . . It was that love, that no matter what I love you." That love provides a safety net—knowing they will be loved whether they succeed or fail.

Further, as we work toward an entrepreneurial culture, we must embrace uncertainty.[7] Margaret J. Wheatley talks about being "willing to be disturbed," that is, being willing to have our ideas and beliefs challenged by others. The application to entrepreneurial culture is profound. Wheatley said,

> We weren't trained to admit we don't know. Most of us were taught to sound certain and confident, to state our opinion as if it were true. We haven't been rewarded for being confused. Or for asking more questions rather than giving quick answers. . . . We can't be creative if we refuse to be confused. Change always starts with confusion. . . . Great ideas and inventions miraculously appear in the space of not knowing.

If we can move through the fear and enter the abyss, we are rewarded greatly. We rediscover we're creative.[8]

The message is powerful; we will find innovation if we embrace not knowing. We may have to sit in the uncertainty for a while before we find the answer. It's a hard place to be as an individual, and it's a hard place to be as an organization, but being comfortable with not having all the answers is critical for benefiting from an entrepreneurial culture. Survivors have navigated uncertainty and have demonstrated resilience in ways that should be admired and can certainly be encouraged in an entrepreneurial culture.

Survivors have navigated uncertainty and have demonstrated resilience in ways that should be admired and can certainly be encouraged in an entrepreneurial culture.

Researchers also found eliminating red tape and the burden of bureaucracy is key to creating an entrepreneurial culture.[9] Nothing kills entrepreneurs' drive for innovation faster than another rule they have to follow, hurdle they have to jump, or guideline they have to dodge.

Ample research, across multiple organizations and industries, has found autonomy is a critical component of a successful entrepreneurial environment.[10] Micromanagement kills innovation. Individuals and organizations funding new ventures have to balance support or guidance and autonomy. Corporations supporting entrepreneurship will perhaps struggle with this even more. When an organization is providing the funding for a project, the temptation is to intervene, but ensuring the entrepreneur feels ownership will result in more successful projects. It is a fragile balance between steering away from failure and letting someone learn from their mistakes. To determine what risk you are willing to assume, perform a cost-benefit analysis before the start of the project. Determine the level of anticipated mistake that requires an intervention and the level of mistake that can be tolerated for learning. For small mistakes, the risk will be worth the reward.

Specific to women overcoming challenging pasts, autonomy is a critical element of entrepreneurial culture. Whether you work with an organization supporting women with challenging pasts or are hiring them, if you operate under the assumption that they cannot act autonomously, everyone will be disadvantaged. The women will not be able to thrive independently without the trust and belief that they have the skill and abilities needed to succeed. We talk about this issue in much greater detail in chapter 4, which covers the translation factor principle. You saw evidence of it in chapter 1 with experiential learning and encouraging overcomers to figure it out. Survivors often lack self-esteem and self-worth. To help them build a self-belief that they can do a task and achieve greater accomplishments, it is critical to demonstrate trust in their abilities and to give them the autonomy to learn.

Finally, a reward system is important for encouraging an entrepreneurial culture: rewards along the way and at the conclusion of successful projects. Rewards could be monetary, but it's not necessary. Rewards can include opportunities to pursue additional projects of interest. Rewards can include celebrations of success along the way, such as incubators or organizations celebrating business openings, first sales, hiring employees, or recovery of capital. For women overcomers, small rewards along the way are critical to building self-esteem and self-worth. They will benefit greatly from celebrating milestones professionally and personally.

Creating an Entrepreneurial Culture

Although every area within an organization can benefit from creative problem-solving and innovative ideas, not every area can be as open to an entrepreneurial spirit. There are some functional areas where things actually have to be done a certain way or, at least, where managers of a unit think they have to be done a certain way (I am looking at you rule-followers!). The following questions can help eliminate functional areas of business units where an entrepreneurial culture would not be a natural fit.

- Where in the organization would failure be too costly?
- Where do we not have enough resources to support innovation?

- What projects require guidelines, especially those set by an external compliance organization, to be followed carefully (i.e., health and safety, tax, and financial reporting)?
- What areas are functioning well and do not need to be disrupted?

A profitable business unit at its peak, for example, would not be the right area to take risks. That business unit might not be in need of innovative ideas. As an accountant, Shannon can say that *creative* and *accounting* should not be used in the same sentence. Areas where a great deal of compliance is needed are not ripe for an entrepreneurial culture. Sure, new ideas are needed in those areas, problems need to be solved, but the rules, regulations, and constraints within those areas will crush the entrepreneurial spirit.

However, a fledgling business unit, with nothing to lose, in need of innovation is often a good place to turn lose the entrepreneurial spirit. The following questions can help identify areas prime for an injection of entrepreneurial culture.

- What processes or tasks are open for innovation or improvement?
- Which departments develop new products?
- What areas of the organization need to be rethought?
- Where is there nothing to lose (i.e., are there failing areas that need innovation)?
- Which managers are better at providing support and tolerating uncertainty?
- What projects can tolerate more risk (and may need more reward)?

AND SO IT BEGINS

Emmie could not get back to the Dream Center fast enough. But she had several appointments in town related to starting her business. *Starting my business?!*, she thought to herself. *I have appointments, so I can start my business.* She couldn't wait to tell Jessica that she was approved for a loan. And not just the loan she asked for but even more. Of course, it would stretch the payback period, requiring more time to pay back the loan. But with the extra $2,000 she could be up and running and making money faster.

"I did it! I did it!" Emmie screamed when she got to the Dream Center.

Jessica flung herself across the room wrapping Emmie in the biggest bear hug ever. The excitement in the room was electric and all the other women working on projects tapped into the energy. Everyone was motivated. Two women from the streets made it. They were making their dreams a reality. Not only that, but they were also only a few months ahead of the rest of the women hoping to live a good life. If Emmie could launch a business only five months after leaving the crack house, why couldn't they?

For the next two weeks, Emmie worked long hours in the space above Carter's, her space, her shop. She would send her kids off to school and drive straight to the shop. She sanded and painted and cleaned and scrubbed. She would leave to get her kids from school, bring them back to the shop, where they worked on homework and played while she kept working. Often, they would fall asleep on the couches that would become the cozy sitting spaces for her future customers, and Emmie would work late into the night. Some nights, Ms. Gloria, the house mom at Hope House, would pick the kids up from school so Emmie could work without distractions.

About two weeks after getting approved, Emmie got the call from the bank. The LRT had partnered with the local bank to provide the loans. They used the money designated for microloans as collateral for lending. This enabled the women to get the loan from a bank instead of the nonprofit Dream Center. It also meant the Dream Center didn't have to navigate all the regulations of the lending industry. Roseanne Martinez was the loan officer and called to tell Emmie her loan was ready, and she could come in and sign the papers at her convenience. Fifteen minutes later, Emmie was sitting in Roseanne's office.

After signing what seemed like hundreds of forms, Roseanne leaned over to hand her the check and said, "Congratulations, here's the check."

"Wait, what? You are giving me the check?" blurted Emmie.

Roseanne replied, "Of course, it is your business."

Emmie looked at the check and looked at Roseanne. Finally, she opened the backpack she always carried and asked Roseanne to drop it inside. She didn't even want to touch the envelope. She thought, *for a recovering addict, the money inside is dangerous.* As she left the office, she turned to look back at Roseanne with a half-smile and thanked her for all her help.

Emmie's mind raced. *What are they thinking? Did that lady just give a $5,000 check to a crack addict? I need to get rid of this fast.* As fast as she rushed to sign the papers, she rushed back even faster to Agnes's office to give her the check. Because many of the women applying for these microloans were women in recovery, the Dream Center required the money be managed by the program director of the Hope House. Agnes would order and pay for whatever materials were outlined in the business plan approved by the LRT. Emmie was more than happy to let her do that part. She knew how dangerous it would be for her, being only five months sober and having access to that much cash.

Two months later, after working every single day, it was finally time for the soft opening of Coffee and Bananas. Emmie and the two women she hired from the Dream Center arrived at 4:00 a.m. to get everything ready for the 6:00 a.m. opening. Fresh brewed coffee and maple banana muffins along with other pastries filled the room with delicious mouthwatering smells. Carol and Agnes were both there to help support Emmie. At 5:55 a.m. Emmie stood at the door of her shop, so excited she was sure she would pee her pants. With trembling fingers, she unlocked and opened her doors.

The lines were long, and people mingled around looking at all the options for art projects that could be purchased. Each art project came in a large plastic bag or box. They contained all the materials and instructions needed to create so many fun crafts. There were projects for kids of all ages from toddlers to high school. Everyone was excited, and Emmie was selling as fast as she could. Around 3:00 p.m. the last customer left, the doors were closed, and the team all gathered together to celebrate an amazing job.

For the first few months, business was great. Emmie worked every day except Sundays. Her kids would join her after school and do art projects and homework until it was time to go to Hope House for dinner. Every single day that Emmie walked out of her shop she would smile and want to pinch herself that she was running her own successful business. Oh, it was hard for sure, but not anywhere as hard as it was trying to survive on the streets. Carol told her early on, "You used to chase dope. Now you just need to chase your dreams." She was right. Emmie was living a dream.

WHY ENTREPRENEURIAL CULTURE WORKS

Entrepreneurial culture works for individuals, organizations (nonprofit and for-profit), and communities. The United Nations Sustainable Development Goal (SDG) number eight, which we will discuss in more detail in the final chapter of this book, sets out to create "Decent work and economic growth." The goal goes on to state, "Sustained and inclusive economic growth can drive progress, create decent jobs for all and improve living standards."[11] Entrepreneurship is one of the greatest tools for economic development and a valuable instrument for unlocking economic growth and improving employment rates.[12] Investment in entrepreneurial endeavors can help us, as a world, fight unemployment and poverty. In the introduction, we further argued the investment is even greater when made in women. Investing in women provides a better return because they will in turn spend money earned bettering their family's health and education, which provides returns for generations and generations. Investment in women not only lifts entire families and entire communities, but it also lifts a mountain of burdens from women's shoulders. All women carry many burdens for their family's financial well-being, physical health, safety, and care. Women have so many jobs in and out of the home doing paid and more often unpaid (or underpaid) labor, such as caring for family members.[13] Women overcoming challenging pasts carry those burdens and more.

The burdens women overcomers carry are better explained in a beautiful article, "When All Women Lift," where women in India formed a women's circle (translated *Mahila Mandal*). They banded together to fight violence against women and poverty. When evaluating their work together, one woman said, "When all women lift, the mountain will move." One member described the mountain by saying,

> This mountain of poverty, this mountain of never-ending work, this mountain of violence, of despair; it weighs me down and bows my back, so I can't even see the sky. . . . I've struggled against it all my life. Alone, it's far too heavy to move. . . . But together? With all of us together, there is hope.[14]

We see Emmie already starting to move the mountain in her story.

Her hard work was an investment she made for her family. By watching her work, her children will know a different way forward. They see the investment their mother is making in improving their lives. They are seeing business at work and learning alongside her. Before starting the business, Emmie was untapped potential. She was not making a significant contribution to society. With the investment from the LRT, she has the potential to lift her community by creating jobs and contributing to the economy.

Wouldn't it be great to be part of moving the mountain? As you saw with Emmie's story so far and will see as it concludes, "together, there is hope." Together requires business leaders to support entrepreneurial culture either through organizations like the LRT within nonprofits or through large organizations.

Supporting Women's Entrepreneurial Efforts

If you are a business leader, or working toward becoming a business leader, you have expertise and influence that can help move the mountain. You have the ability to invest in ideas of women like Emmie, either financially or with your time through mentorship. You have seen many people in Emmie's story make a difference. So far, you have met Jessica, a peer who mentored her, the staff of the organization providing housing and emotional support, the group at the Dream Center providing training, Robert and Tom along with other members of the LRT who were not named, Carter's Plumbing that provided space for the shop and mentorship through business incubation, First Union Bank that facilitated funding, and Roseanne the loan officer. You will meet more business mentors in the next section. Who will you be in the story of a woman in recovery, like Emmie? What role will you play?

Hiring Women into Entrepreneurial Culture

If you are a supervisor, you can hire women overcoming challenging pasts. You can work to understand what they need from their supervisor and to develop an entrepreneurial culture in your organization where they can thrive. Your company will benefit at the same time. In the presence of the entrepreneurial culture, women overcomers bring nontraditional and diverse ideas to the organization. They can develop new products and services employees with more traditional pasts could not imagine. Organizations that fully embrace an entrepreneurial culture will benefit from the resourcefulness, resilience, and "hustle" women who have overcome challenging pasts have honed.

GROWING AND GROWING PAINS

Stacks of files and papers covered every inch of the small desk in the back corner of Emmie's office at her shop. Tears rolled down her cheeks as she reread the letter from the IRS. Her failure to pay taxes on time resulted in significant fines. How could she be so stupid? She knew she had to pay taxes, but she thought it would be at the end of the year. She didn't know she had to pay quarterly, at least not until this fourth quarter.

She barely had the money to pay the fines. If she paid it in full, she would not have the funds to hire the new employee she desperately needed. Emmie was so excited that she was going to hire another employee because that meant she would have more time with her children in the afternoon. Now, because of this, she would have to continue working long hours. She worked so hard and now money was just being wasted because of her stupid mistake. As she sat there crying, a vibration in her pocket stirred her from her melancholy. She looked at her phone, and it was Harrison Calvin. Harrison was a businessman who frequented Coffee and Bananas. He said he was obsessed with her maple banana muffins. Emmie didn't want to answer, but she knew she should.

"Hey Emmie, how's it going?" Harrison asked.

It was common for him to call from time to time. He had become her unofficial business mentor and was always checking on her and encouraging her. She wanted to tell him that everything was good so he wouldn't know what a failure she was. But it would be a lie. So, she told him what happened. After sharing her woes, he told her to stop by his office in a few hours, and they would talk about how to move forward.

Three hours later she was sitting in his office. He suggested they call the IRS and see what her options were. He knew who to contact, so they made the call together. The call with the IRS was surprisingly productive. Although she did have to pay the fines, the agent on the phone set up a payment plan for her that was doable. Thankfully, now she could hire that new employee.

After the call, Harrison asked her "Do you know what makes a good businessperson?" Emmie gave several answers: hardworking, creative, responsible, entrepreneurial. Harrison nodded and said all those things were important.

But he added, "What really makes a good businessperson is getting up and going back at it after a failure."

"Well crap, then I am the most excellent businessperson ever! I have been failing and starting over my whole life" grinned Emmie.

The shop was packed with customers when Emmie returned from Harrison's office. There were tables with moms and their kids doing arts and crafts. College students were huddled together in study groups and businesspeople in meetings. Emmie felt a burst of pride as she glanced around. She had done this. She dreamed up Coffee and Bananas, and here it was a booming success despite her failures.

But she quickly realized it was not just due to her own hard work because she had so much help along the way: Jessica, the LRT, Harrison, her kids, and her employees. They all played a role in the success. Emmie decided she could do the same thing. She could help other women live their dreams. She contacted the local workforce to submit a job opening. She also called Agnes to tell her there was an opening at Coffee and Bananas for a full-time barista. Agnes happened to have a woman in her office at the moment who was so frustrated she had been unable to find a job.

"Send her over for an interview," Emmie said.

An hour later, Mechelle was in her office filling out an application. They talked for a few minutes, and Mechelle explained her background check would show several felony drug charges. Emmie reassured Mechelle that it didn't matter. Emmie shared her background with Mechelle and reiterated that everyone deserved second, third, fourth, and fiftieth chances in life. Seeing Mechelle let out a breath and sink a little into her chair with a smile was enough for Emmie.

"The job is yours if you want it? When can you start?"

Mechelle sat up like a bolt and blurted out, "Now!"

Emmie laughed and said they were only open for another hour and she could start tomorrow. They went through the details of filling out forms and going over expectations. Mechelle left with her new uniform in hand. She nearly skipped as she left the office. Emmie knew then and there that she would always try to hire women that needed a chance. Just like someone had trusted her when she was the most untrustworthy, she would do the same for others.

A year later, Mechelle was the store manager and did an amazing job keeping everything running smoothly. Having Mechelle take over so many responsibilities allowed Emmie to dream about what might come next. Emmie started her days opening Coffee and Bananas. She loved early mornings, when she felt most productive. Mechelle would come in midmorning and work until closing. Most days Emmie had various lunch meetings to network and explore ways to grow her business. Today was an exciting day. Emmie's latest adventure was the creation of Businesses United for Good or BUG as she liked to call it. BUG was a group of local businesses that wanted to help the community. Today would be their second meeting. After getting to know each other at the last meeting, today, Emmie was going to talk about hiring higher-risk employees like she and Mechelle had been.

As the group settled, Emmie started the conversation by asking her fellow business owners, "How willing would you be to hire someone with felonies and known drug issues?"

Most said they would and some actually had, but it had gone poorly. Emmie expected that concern. So, with a sly smile, Emmie asked, "How willing would you be to hire me?" She spent the next forty-five minutes sharing about her past and what worked and didn't work. She talked to the business owners about their responsibility to understand the specific issues employees with nontraditional pasts, like hers, face.

When the meeting ended, the group decided the next step was to create a training manual from all their experiences with high-risk employees and look at best practices on retaining and tapping into the amazing resources those employees actually bring to the workplace. They decided the first step was that BUG would hire a part-time employee to compile all the information and produce a manual. Emmie loved the idea but reminded everyone that BUG was just a network and they had no money.

Karen Marthiljohni, owner of a large oil and gas company said, "I can take care of this part. I'll underwrite that cost."

"Are you serious?" Emmie asked.

Karen whipped out her checkbook and said, "Indeed, I am and here's the check."

Emmie looked at the check in Karen's hand and saw the amount was for $50,000.

Eyes bulging, Emmie asked, "Are you serious? That is so much."

Karen went on to explain she was serious but wanted the group to hire someone who needed a second or fiftieth chance. And that person deserved a fair, living wage. Emmie couldn't hold back the tears. This time she didn't ask Karen to drop the check in her bag. Emmie just grabbed it and responded, "Indeed! Here's the check!"

4

PEEKING IN WINDOWS

Translation Factor

How pathetic is your life when your favorite pastime is to peek into windows of people's houses when you walk down the street at night?

Peeking in windows was a mixed bag for Maggie. She loved to see all the pretty rooms and nice furniture. The warm yellow glow in some homes seemed so cozy and safe. Maggie liked houses where the rooms were bright, and everything was shiny. It made her feel clean just looking in from the outside. She dreamed of what it would be like to live in a safe, clean home. One minute she smiled as she imagined what it was like to live in one of the homes, and the next minute, she swallowed the realization that tonight she had no home and would sleep in her usual spot behind the dumpster at the end of Spence St. Her husband B. B. was in jail and that meant she had no place to stay until he got out.

As she walked down the street, her mind drifted back to the time when she was about to turn twelve. Her family lived in a the small two-bedroom house in Carterville. It was tiny with cracks in the windows and holes in the wood under the sinks in the kitchen and bedroom. She had the small room that was converted from a storage closet to her bedroom. Her four brothers shared the real bedroom.

Maggie loved her room. There was just enough space for the twin mattress on the floor and a little dresser.

She remembered the day when everything changed. It was three days from her twelfth birthday. Her greatest concern when the day started was whether one of her birthday presents would be the new shoes she so desperately wanted that matched the ones that the rich White girls had in her class. She was sitting with her legs crossed trying to decide if she wanted to draw or go next door and hang out with Felix, her best friend, when her mother opened the door.

Her mom stared out the window and said quietly, "It's time for a Sancho. And I have someone who is ready."

Maggie's eyes bulged, and her jaw dropped. She couldn't believe what she was hearing. She knew what a Sancho was. He would be some dirty old man who would take pictures of her naked and maybe even do other stuff that she found even thinking about terrifying.

"Mom, you can't do that. I don't want a Sancho." Maggie said as her cheeks flushed red.

"Well, it's not your choice. I have already arranged it. He will be here Friday. End of discussion," spat her mother as she turned and walked away.

Friday afternoon, her mother opened Maggie's bedroom door and stepped aside to let Hector Ramirez in the room. He handed Maggie's mother some money as she walked away and closed the door. Hector just stared at Maggie for the first few minutes. Finally, he asked her if she knew what to do. She didn't budge. He went on to say that she needed to undress, and he was just going to take a few pictures. She couldn't figure out why her fingers were unbuttoning her shirt. That was the last thing she wanted to do. Her fingers must have known there was no point fighting. This was her Sancho. Her mother had a Sancho growing up, and so did her grandmother. This was just the way it was.

She stood and removed her shorts and sat back down on the bed. Hector pulled out his phone and began snapping pictures. Several times he told her to get into different poses and then snap, snap, snap. Several times he told her to smile, but she refused. *I may have to let you do this, but you can't make me smile like I am happy.* She realized that day that some things happened to her, but she would decide how and what she would do despite it. Maggie figured he must have taken hundreds of pictures. Finally, he smiled, thanked her, and said he would be back in a few days.

That was the first of many meetings with Hector in that back room. It wasn't long before pictures were not enough, and every time Hector expected more, Maggie complied. Her tiny room no longer felt like the cozy one it once was. It became the place where a little piece of her died each time Hector opened the door. But she also learned how to get what she wanted from Hector. Before long, not only was he paying her mom for his "visits," but he was also bringing Maggie gifts. He always brought her favorite wine coolers. And it was super easy for her to convince him to bring her new clothes because she modeled them for him. If he was going to take from her, she would take from him.

When Maggie was fifteen years old, she met Brandon Brown at a family barbecue in her backyard. He went by the name Big Bullet, but he told Maggie she could call him B. B. Maggie saw him and thought he was the hottest guy she had ever seen. His eyes moved from her face to her body, back to her face, and a huge grin flashed across his face. Then another woman caught his eye. It was on. Maggie knew how to get what she wanted, and she wanted B. B. Before he had a chance to speak to the other woman, Maggie was by his side. She knew exactly what to do to get a guy. She knew guys needed to think it was their idea. By the time she was fifteen, she had mastered the art of manipulation. She knew how to get extra cash off her Sancho that her mom never knew about, and she knew how to get B. B. to "pick her up." A few hours later they were at his place and spent the next few hours drinking, smoking weed, and making out. Sometime in the middle of the night Maggie dozed off. Her head was on B. B.'s chest and she never felt safer or more loved than she did in that moment. It didn't matter that it started as a game for her or that she just met him. She knew she was in love and hoped he felt the same way.

That was five years ago, and Maggie never left his side. Well, at least when he was not in jail or with some other chick. She hated it when he went after other women, but he always came back to her. He should make bond soon, but until then, Maggie slept outside. It is not like they had a house when he was out. Mainly they stayed in run-down, rent-by-the-week motels. Fortunately, Maggie had B. B.'s phone so she could keep in touch with her Johns. Maggie had the numbers memorized. She had always been good with numbers. When she needed dope, she pulled out the phone. Some days, no one would answer, and Maggie would be stuck sitting on the curb or walking to another dope house to see if she could find someone to front her until she got cash.

Today was one of those days, so Maggie decided to head to Angelo's—the closest crack house. As she was walking, she heard the sound she dreaded. She could hear a school bus coming for blocks—something about the way the tires hummed on the asphalt in the hot Texas heat and the sound of the kids chattering beside open windows. As the bus approached, Maggie dropped her head and let her hair fall to the sides of her face. She hated the way the kids on the bus looked at her. She was sure they saw her as the trashy homeless street lady, who nobody loved.

She got to Angelo's and thankfully he agreed to front her some dope. She needed it. Just when the edge was gone, the phone buzzed in her pocket. She pulled it out and saw it was the county jail. She knew what that meant: B. B. was out.

Stabbing the phone, she said, "Baby, are you out?"

His smooth voice and sweet words confirmed he was, and she was so excited.

Angelo agreed to take her to the jail to pick him up. After that, B. B. called in some favors and got enough money to get a room at a seedy motel. She was lying on the bed enjoying the AC when she felt the tingles on her neck. She just flashed her hand under her hair, and sure enough, a roach fluttered off her fingers onto the floor. Roaches stopped bothering her a long time ago. They were the permanent residents at that motel. Maggie and B. B. were just their guests.

B. B. took his cell phone from Maggie and began to make calls. Maggie asked him to stop.

"Baby, you just got out. Let's just spend this one night together, alone," she begged.

B. B. waved his hand in the air and kept making calls. Before long, several of his guys and their girls were piled on the bed. Felecia came with Hector. Felecia was probably the closest thing Maggie had to a friend. As close as a friend can be, anyway, when loyalties are to crack first. When dope started to run out, friends got hard core. She remembered the time she was getting high with another friend and the dope ran out. They went on a drug run but didn't get as much as expected. So, her friend stabbed Maggie in the neck and took off. That "friend" cost her fifteen stitches and a night in the ER. At least Felecia never stabbed her. So even though she liked Felecia, she had hoped it would just be her and B. B. tonight.

As she sat there fuming, she heard B. B. tell one of the guys to go book the room next to them, and Maggie's stomach dropped. She knew what that meant. B. B. walked over to her and handed her a joint. She hit it hard. Somebody had brought a large bottle of Ancient Age whiskey that Maggie grabbed and poured into a plastic cup.

Five minutes later, the door to the connected room opened. B. B. looked at her and looked at the open door. Maggie knew what to do. She chugged the whiskey, poured a second glass to the top, and went to the next room. Stepping inside she realized it had not been cleaned from the last person. The sheets were on the floor, there was trash on the tables, and cups with golden fluid that floated cigarette butts. Maggie loved B. B. and considered him her husband. She would do anything for him, even if that meant heading to the other room. However, no one else in the room saw their relationship the same way. Everyone else knew B. B. was her pimp, and he had her wrapped. She took off her shorts and laid on the bed and waited. She knew what was coming. She didn't know who was coming, but she knew what.

Felecia pretended not to notice Maggie leaving. Instead, Felecia focused on why she was there and continued to smoke for hours until the sun began to show in the window. All night while they got high, one man after another would come in, give B. B. some cash, and then head to the joining room. Felecia got up to go to the bathroom as another guy was handing B. B. cash. As she walked past the open door to the other room, she saw Maggie curled in a ball. Even with the dim light barely coming through the windows, Felecia could see the yellow and brown stains on the nasty mattress with no sheets. She also saw Maggie staring into the darkness. Just as Felecia stepped into the bathroom, the next man went into Maggie's room. He didn't even bother to shut the door. None of them did. Felecia brushed the disgust out of her mind and went back to the dope. Too much to think about.

The whiskey was not enough to numb Maggie. She was not high enough. She could smell every guy that came in. Most of them were sweaty and smelled like cigarettes, whiskey, and dope. Every now and then some Romeo wannabe came in clearly freshly showered and wearing cologne. But it didn't matter. To her they were all dirty. And if they were dirty, then what was she?

Eventually the stream of men stopped. Sometime later that afternoon Felecia realized Maggie was sitting next to her getting high as well. When their eyes caught, Maggie exhaled a long stream of smoke. No words were needed. Last night it was Maggie, another night it would be Felecia's turn. They both knew the routine. Most people would look at Maggie and Felecia and think they were weak and easily manipulated. But they were tough. Maggie knew she was tough. She had to be to survive the trail of men. Little did she know how valuable that would be for her one day. But in the meantime, now that it was over, there was nothing more to do but smoke until she crashed and burned—which was exactly what Maggie did.

TRANSLATION FACTOR

Much about Maggie's background is devastating, but if we look closely at her story, we can see some skills and attributes Maggie gained from overcoming so much. The fourth principle—translation factor—involves helping women overcomers translate those skills and attributes into the workplace.

What Is Translation Factor?

Through translation factor, a mentor should "acknowledge and value the attributes and skills" someone gained through typically marginalized experiences and encourage translation of those attributes and skills to be effective in lawful work.[1] In an article, titled "Learn How to Hustle for Good," Shannon and her research colleagues provided evidence for the effectiveness of translation factor strategy.

Cheryl used translation factor in the housing program she ran to support women transitioning from challenging pasts to a completely different future.

As Shannon and her colleagues found, the biggest challenge women faced when first exiting was a lack of self-worth or self-esteem—meaning valuing themselves. Their lack of self-esteem also created a lack of self-efficacy—a lack of belief in their abilities—in their ability to sustain a more mainstream lifestyle and job. The lack of belief in themselves impacted their personal and their professional lives. Job self-efficacy specifically applies to beliefs about one's ability to perform at work. When low, such a mindset prevents someone from believing they can use their skills to secure or maintain a job.[2]

Efficacy is important because it can affect how well we perform at work, and it can influence our career choice.[3] So, low job self-efficacy, especially when it is based on misinformation, can have a significant negative impact on someone's career. When first exiting a challenging past, most women have low job self-efficacy. They do not believe in their ability to perform well in lawful employment. Even if they believe they have skills, they do not believe they can apply these skills well in a traditional work environment.

Again, low self-efficacy can occur even when someone has valuable skills. Specific to women exiting the sex trade, the scholars found that their ability to hustle and motivate, as well as their resourcefulness and resilience, were critical skills and attributes the women developed in their time in the sex trade. In the first section of Maggie's story, we see her resilience and ability to survive overwhelming situations. When first exiting, the women associate these skills and attributes with negative beliefs about themselves. They need someone to help them recognize these same skills can be used in business with a small amount of translation.

Requirements for Translation Factor

The first requirement for translation factor is to have supervisors or coaches who will acknowledge the skills and attributes employees with marginalized pasts gained through previous experiences. The experiences may have been illegal or nontraditional, but they contributed to the unique portfolio the women bring to a job. One participant said the following about receiving help to translate her ability to hustle into a marketable skill:

> She always tells us . . . you used to hustle for money, back in them days for bad. Now you need to learn how to hustle for good. You used to make sure you had your contacts in place and you knew who was giving money from what time to what. You need to know what you need to take care of over here. She's right. And I know how to do that. I just have to move it . . . for good.[4]

First, acknowledge the ability.

The second requirement is for supervisors or coaches to help survivors translate those skills for use in lawful employment. Another participant described the power of a trusted mentor implementing the translation factor. The participant described the mentor saying:

> "You weren't given a set of skills to be a crackhead prostitute. You can take those same attributes." She called them attributes. I had never called them that. I had always said, "I'm super manipulative. I get what I want. I'm pushy and bossy." And she said, "All of those things translate well into business and here's what they look like." And I needed somebody to tell me that . . . I've always been able to manipulate people. I use it in a good way now. It's motivation now as opposed to manipulation.[5]

The participant did not know the attribute she had viewed as so negative could be turned into a positive in business until a mentor pointed it out to her.

According to Shannon's research, translation factor was the most important principle, and it is an enhancing principle. It enhances the impact of the other principles, especially experiential learning and immediate leadership opportunity, and conversely they enhance the impact of translation factor. In fact, firsthand, personal experiences have been found most effective in improving self-efficacy. These experiences can be gained through experiential learning and immediate leadership.

However, the benefits of experiential learning are magnified when an overcomer realizes an influential person views them positively.[6] This phenomenon is called *reflected efficacy*, which is the role someone else's beliefs about us have on what we believe about ourselves. How other people view us influences how we view ourselves. This is because we learn what other people believe about us through relationships. The overcomers we know had been viewed negatively by others most of their adult lives. Positive growth-promoting relationships at work—such as those with coaches, mentors, or supervisors—can significantly impact a person's self-efficacy or belief in themselves.

Creating the Translation Factor

What elements need to be in place to implement translation factor effectively? What areas in the business are most prime for translation factor? The good news is translation factor can be used anywhere to encourage and support employees, especially those with nontraditional career paths. In fact, for many women overcoming challenging pasts, it may be the first time anyone values their past. This is critical because some of those skills and attributes will be unique to a survivor and likely not held by someone who had a more traditional path. The diversity in skills and attributes can be so valuable to companies.

In fact, for many women overcoming challenging pasts, it may be the first time anyone values their past.

The following questions could help companies identify the areas where they could benefit from translation factor the most.

- Which areas of our business are staffed with encouraging supervisors who could respect nontraditional skills or attributes?
- Which departments could benefit from training supervisors to be more encouraging of people's strengths and past experiences?
- Which nontraditional skills or attributes could translate into business skills we need in our organization?
- Which employees in our organization currently could benefit from someone recognizing their prior experiences as "legitimate and transferable."[7]

- Which supervisors are particularly good coaches?
- Which departments could benefit from formal training in recognizing others' strengths (look for departments where staff are underperforming)?

Because supervisors play such a critical role in translation factor, many of these questions relate to the way supervisors interact with employees.

In fact, Cheryl interacted with a company that was looking to hire marginalized employees. They had started a program that would bring in a team with nontraditional educational paths. They wanted Cheryl to come in to train the employees. She said no, but she would be glad to come in to train the supervisors to better understand these potential nontraditional employees. If a company is struggling to successfully employ marginalized employees, they likely need to train supervisors in translation factor.

STEPPING OUT

Two years later, B. B. was arrested again. Maggie had gone to the store and when she got home, B. B. was gone. The next day, still no B. B., but she wasn't too worried. He did this all the time. She just hoped he was getting high or picking up more dope and not in bed with some slut. Around four that afternoon, she heard that B. B. and several other guys he ran with were arrested for aggravated assault and robbery. There were rumors of an attempted murder charge. The night of the arrest, they went to pick up a drop from a dealer named Froggy and things went bad. B. B. thought he was getting robbed and pulled out his 9 mm and shot Froggy. Shots started flying and several hit B. B.'s car and tires. Froggy's girlfriend was in his car. B. B. grabbed her by the hair, yanked her out of the passenger seat, and hit her on the head with his gun, and they all stole the car. Nobody died that night, but Froggy was in ICU for several days.

Police were on the scene before B. B. got more than a block away. Five cop cars chased B. B. and his friends. They tried to make a sharp turn to get away and instead ended up in the fence of someone's yard. They all jumped out to run, but it was no use. The cops were on them. Thirty minutes later, they were handcuffed in the back of the police car.

Once Maggie heard how things went down, she was beside herself. This did not look good for B. B. And sure enough, it was not. A month later, Maggie picked up the phone on the side of the booth in the visitation room at the jail. B. B. sat on the other side of the glass with the phone to his ear. His fingers traced the hundreds of scratched initials on the metal shelf in front of him. He couldn't look at Maggie as he told her the district attorney was sticking them with a laundry list of charges and seeking life.

Instantly tears rolled as she cried, "No, baby, Nooooooo. Please tell me that's not right."

Looking up he said, "I can't. This is what my attorney told me this morning."

What was she going to do? How could she live without her man? What was going to happen to her? She tried to talk but just sat there and cried. Eventually, the guards announced visitation was over and they had to leave. Maggie and B. B. leaned and touched their foreheads together from opposite sides of the glass as they placed the phones back on the wall.

Maggie knew she needed to find a place to stay. The first person she called was Harold. He was one of her regulars. He lived alone, and she was pretty sure he would let her crash on his couch. He was hesitant at first and told her she could only stay a few days. But Maggie knew how to work men, and before the end of the week, she had a permanent(ish) place in Harold's home and bed. It wasn't perfect but it was better than the streets.

Four months later, Maggie felt sick and knew something was wrong. She had missed her period but assumed she couldn't get pregnant. The next day the nausea was worse, and the pregnancy test she bought on a whim was positive. She was going to have Harold's baby. Maggie was delighted. It didn't matter that the baby was Harold's. It only mattered that she was going to have a tiny person who would love her. Harold was not so happy. When he found out he lost it. He said he knew it was not his, and she had to get her %@#$ ass out of his house.

Maggie grabbed a trash bag and threw in shoes, clothes, and what little toiletries Harold would let her take and left. Now what was she going to do? She knew how to make it on the streets but not while she was pregnant. Even if she could make it, she didn't want her baby born on the streets. She decided to call Felecia and see if she could crash at her place. Felecia was excited to hear from Maggie but told her she was living in a sober home.

"Maggie, you need to come here. They will help you. This place is good." Felecia said.

The more Maggie thought about it the more it made sense. Why not try to make a better life? She was going to be a mom, and she needed to find a way to take care of her baby. Of course, she never worked a real job her entire life, but that didn't mean she couldn't get one. The next day, she was signing the rental agreement for her new place in the sober living home. When Maggie walked through the door, Felecia greeted her with a hug. They spent the rest of the afternoon catching up and talking about what was next for both of them.

Felecia told Maggie about a new program offered through the Community Action Committee (CAC) called Work Better. Typically, the CAC provided resources to meet gaps people experienced, like paying a light bill or rental assistance, but recently they added this new program called Work Better and offered courses on how to increase employability and earning potential. They partnered with a consortium of local businesses so that upon graduation candidates could be hired in a variety of industries earning good money. Maggie immediately signed up for courses.

Felecia had graduated from Work Better but instead of being hired at one of the consortium businesses, the executive director of CAC convinced her to join the team at Work Better. Felecia ended up being Maggie's supervisor in the first training program she completed. Maggie was shocked when she saw how professional Felecia dressed and acted at work. It was completely different from the Felecia she knew at the home and *way* different from the Felecia she knew from the dope house. Maggie was given a packet with assignments to work on. The work was hard, but Maggie loved every minute of it. She also loved the way baby Zachary kicked as she worked. It wouldn't be long, and she would be a momma. She needed to work hard so she could get a good job.

Maggie flew through the first two sections of the course work for Work Better. She was excited to start the third phase, until she got the details about it. Her first assignment was to create a pilot program for a new training. It could be any kind of training, but the assignment included details about the course content and a budget, including a spreadsheet for tracking. Felecia explained, if the plan was good, and they ended up using it, Maggie might get a stipend from the money it generated. Maggie had no idea how to create a pilot program, much less a budget and a spreadsheet. She followed Felecia to her office asking what she needed to do. Felecia answered the way she always answered, "Figure it out." It was one thing learning about computers and Word, but this was way bigger. Maggie asked Felecia again for at least some directions.

Again, Felicia laughed and said, "You can figure it out."

Maggie read through the material. The numbers came a little more naturally to her, so she started on the budget and the tracking spreadsheet. Eventually, she would have to figure out how to sell the course. The assignment packet mentioned marketing strategies, but she didn't know what those did. So, she did what everyone else did at Work Better, she googled it. As she read, she realized she had to create a plan that would convince people to pay for the new training. She had no idea how to convince people to buy something. This was stupid. Why did they think she knew how to do this? Walking back into Felecia's office, Maggie flopped her big belly into the chair.

"Felecia, I have no idea how to convince people to buy something, let alone a training." Maggie whined. Followed by several minutes of ongoing whining about how this was too much for her and to give her a different assignment.

When she was finished with her rant, Felecia asked her if she ever manipulated a guy to give her something she wanted. Maggie laughed and said of course she had. That is how she got most of her stuff because she rarely had her own money.

Smiling, Felicia said, "Well then you know how to do marketing. You knew what to say to get the cash from a guy, this is no different. Just a different context."

Maggie half closed her eyes and half smiled. "You are so sneaky. All right, all right, I will give it a shot." And she did. Two weeks later, Maggie was presenting her marketing strategy to the staff of Work Better. Two weeks after that, Maggie got her stipend for the implementation of her plan. Two weeks after that, baby Zachary came into the world.

WHY TRANSLATION FACTOR WORKS

Translation factor works. Most of us could benefit from the principle. We all have previous experiences that have shaped us into who we are today. Those previous experiences or skills learned can translate into something we can use in our current job. Those aspects of translation factor were even more important for the survivors we interviewed and supported—those with less traditional paths. Many of the women talked about how everyone in their life had given up on them. The world viewed them as failures who did not contribute to society.

When the women encounter someone who validates the experiences, it is shockingly antithetical to their experiences with everyone else. There is power in valuing the characteristics everyone else had told them were downfalls. There is power in translating these skills they thought were so useless—failings of their personalities—into something valued by employers. Examples include validating the management skills women gained in coordinating Johns or drug deals and then translating those skills into managing schedules and appointments in an office. Others need someone to validate their ability to manipulate people and to hustle illegal goods and services. Then they need help translating that into motivating employees, a strong work ethic, and an ability to sell legal goods and services. You see it in phrases from participants like, "She called them attributes. I had never called them that." Others give them a new language to describe what they had only viewed as negative before.

As we stated previously, translation factor works because of a phenomenon called *reflected efficacy*.[8] Shannon and her colleagues found in their study that "reflected efficacy acted as a bridge influencer to overcome the negative attitudes participants had about their existing skills and attributes and the ability to use them to succeed" in lawful employment.[9] When a supervisor showed them it was true, they believed it themselves.

Translation factor can go a long way to increase our self-efficacy. When a respected person in our lives tells us something positive about ourselves, it can have sig-

> When a trusted person told the overcomers they could take the skills they learned on the street and use them in a company, they believed they could—many for the first time.

nificant power. In Cheryl's experiences, because the women value her opinion, when she tells them they can translate their skills and attributes into something marketable to businesses, they believe her. When a trusted person tells the overcomers they can take the skills they learned on the street and use them in a company, they believe they can—many for the first time.

Growth-promoting relationships are important for all of us. They are a lifeline for the women who have been told all their lives that they were not good enough and for the women who thought something was fundamentally wrong with them. Growth-promoting individuals helped them see they already had something that was worthy, and they could use it to achieve new goals.

The result is a new sense of validation—no longer in their ability to attract a John but in their ability to use their intellectual skills. One of the participants called feeling like she was good at the sex trade "a false sense of accomplishment." Another participant said,

> It was also a way I felt validated that I was pretty. Like I always felt attractive when they chose me or something like that. It was really sick. . . . my self-esteem, my self-worth were really wrapped around men finding me attractive in a certain way. . . . Standing on the street corner out there and when the guys drove by and picked you, I was like, "I'm pretty. Gotta go." And no. I mean, I got into so many situations that were horrific thinking they picked me, oh they picked me. And it validated that I was somehow okay or good enough.

She went on to say, accomplishments at work made her no longer need "to be validated, like, 'Oh you're pretty.'" She found her validation in "Oh you're intellectual, oh, you can think."[10]

About the self-worth and self-esteem that comes from working, the same participant talked about feeling validated through work after exiting. She said,

> You start to build self-worth and self-esteem, because you have a job and you're doing something. . . . Having a purpose, feeling needed, feeling like I was doing something productive, like I was a productive member of society . . . and not feeling like I was on the opposite side. Starting to feel like I was on the right side, I think really helped . . . integrate me into society.[11]

Using translation factor to increase overcomers' belief in their ability to work in lawful employment can have a significant impact on their work and life.

DIGGING DEEPER

Maggie learned so much while she studied at Work Better. The most important was that she was smart. When she discovered she had a brain and with a new baby to support, she knew she should go to school, but unfortunately there was no way. And some of her old habits died hard: primarily, the desire to have a man in her life, no matter what type of man that was. For a short while, she dated Kevin but when he stole her daycare money to buy drugs, she knew it would never work. That short relationship resulted in her second son, William.

When she left Kevin, she reached back out to the people at her old sober living house to see if they could help. She found out they had a new housing program to help single moms who were trying to better their futures. This new program allowed her to have her own apartment, but she had to attend college full-time while working part-time. It was the break she needed. She studied hard and got her GED and then enrolled in college. Maggie and the boys lived in a small but nice apartment. Even with the place to live, the budget was so tight. She received funds from her Pell grant, a small check from

Temporary Assistance for Needy Families (TANF), and food stamps that they tried to make sound better by calling it the Supplementary Nutritional Assistance Program (SNAP). But even with all that, she barely made it through each month. Some semesters it was worse, like when the Child Care Management Services funds were not available. She had to visit local food pantries to lower her food bill to pay for daycare. Those semesters, she took fewer hours at college to lower her daycare costs. She was glad when both boys started school. With joy, and a hint of irony, she put her kids on the school bus each morning and remembered the days she knew the kids on the bus were looking at her like a homeless person. Now her boys looked out those windows and saw a mom they loved. And their friends saw her sons' "cool mom."

Despite all that, she graduated. Six years later she graduated with a degree in accounting. She then started working for Kings and Associates. She had done an internship with Kings, and they offered her a great job upon graduation. She loved her work at Kings, and her goal was to make partner. She worked long hours to position herself as a candidate. After long days at work, she still had to go home and make sure she spent quality time with her boys, even if it was a short time before bed. She hired Christina, a nanny, who not only did drop-offs and pick-ups for school but also helped with household chores. Because Christina loved Zac and William so much, it slightly appeased Maggie's guilt for working so much. But if she made partner, things would change.

Maggie was one of three candidates for partner last year. That was a pretty significant accomplishment because she only worked for Kings and Associates for twelve years. The founder, Andrew King, called her in one afternoon a year ago to tell her she was up for partner.

"You are a candidate because you are one of the best accountants we have, not to mention probably the hardest working." Andrew explained as that meeting ended and added, "Someone raised you well."

Maggie smiled as she got up to leave and said, "Not really, but when you go through hard times, like I did, you learn fast how to work hard to make it. I just translated that into my work ethic."

Sadly, she did not make partner. Instead, they gave it to Todd Abernathy. Maggie was crushed when she heard. It would be one thing if the person who made partner was a stronger candidate than her but Todd? There were many evenings Maggie watched Todd head home before her. And from time to time his work crossed her desk for various reasons, and it was not that great. Why? Why Todd and not her? When Maggie first began working at Kings, a coworker warned her about Kings being a good old boys club. Maggie didn't want to believe it, but now she started to realize that indeed that may have been the case.

The Sunday after learning she did not make partner, she was meeting with the associate pastor at her church, Robert Waters. He could tell something was bothering Maggie, and he asked what was going on. She explained about not making partner. Robert seemed sympathetic until she told him how frustrating it was to be a woman in that environment, that she had to work harder than the men in the office, and even then, it didn't pay off.

Robert frowned and said, "Well, I doubt it was just because you are a woman." He then went on to talk about how people didn't always give him opportunities because he was young, so he just worked harder to prove he was capable.

"You just need to work harder," he added.

Maggie was shocked. Did he really say that to her? He had no idea how hard she worked. She tried to explain the issues she faced on a regular basis being a woman in the business world. But clearly Robert had no clue when he said, "Well, I think all those experiences happen to other people, too."

That was it. Maggie's cheeks burned as she said, "Really, you know men with coworkers who comment about how much they like the fit of their sweater, while staring at their boobs? Have you ever had a coworker ask you if it was that 'time of the month' when you disagreed with an approach they were taking?"

Sadly, Robert did not keep his mouth shut and laughed as he added, "Come on, like anyone really has those types of experiences in this day and age."

That was it. Maggie slammed the laptop closed. As she got up to leave, she said, "You do not get to tell me about my experiences as a woman. Geez, I feel sorry for your wife." And she turned and left. That was the last week she attended that church.

For the next year, Maggie focused on work. She had been down before, and every time she overcame. She worked hard for her clients, but she also had a priority to bring in new clients. She had her eye on PDL Industries. PDL was a major manufacturing company opening a plant in their community. All the accounting firms were eager to bring them on as clients. Maggie had great insights and met with the new CEO multiple times.

She could hardly contain her excitement when she got the call. She got the account. Everyone else in the firm was also impressed. Three months later, Maggie got word that she would be compensated with a nice bonus. After the meeting, Andrew asked her how she landed the engagement.

"Just some skills I learned in my former life that came in handy." She smiled as she remembered Felecia's lesson about turning manipulation into motivation and hustle into marketing.

After work Maggie headed home. She decided to use some of her bonus money to take her little family out for a fun evening—dinner and a movie. The boys had been begging her to go to the latest Marvel release. It was dark as she turned in the driveway. Instead of pulling in the garage, she stopped the car and turned off the lights. The blinds in the front windows of her home were open and she could see the boys inside playing monopoly with Christina. Tears rolled down Maggie's cheeks as she watched her boys laugh and play. She may not be a partner at King's, but she was good at her job. Today was proof she was very good at her job. That was enough. And this was her life, those were her boys, and this a home she provided for her family. This time she wasn't looking through someone else's windows, she was at her home peeking in the windows.

5

THIS IS MY LIFE

Restorative Justice

*This is my life. It will never change. It will never get better. I will
never change. I am a heroin addict who will go in and out of prison
for the rest of my life.* Those thoughts bumped through Diana's mind
over and over as she "pulled chain."

Once again, she was arrested and convicted on another felony drug
charge. This was her fifth time to prison. And just like the last four
times, around 2:00 a.m., the guards at the county jail woke her and
several other women who were convicted and sentenced. It was time
to leave county and go to the Department of Corrections. Pulling chain
was not new. She was handcuffed and shackled to Barbara. Barbara
was four feet ten inches, and Diana was almost six feet tall. The height
difference made the whole scene even more ridiculous. As they clinked
their way down the jail corridor to the prison bus, Diana had to lean
down close to Barbara to keep the cuffs from cutting into her wrists.

They drove into the night, headed to the prison unit to begin their
sentence. Diana had been to this unit once before. But her last two
trips to prison were to the Substance Abuse Punishment unit, which
was much better than where they were headed tonight. This was not
going to be good. And Barbara was losing it next to Diana. This was
Barbara's first time to prison, and she was freaking out.

"You need to get your shit together before we get there or those women will eat you up." Diana whispered with disgust to Barbara.

Diana's first trip to prison was when she was only seventeen years old. She had been in and out of juvenile detention for years but was shocked at the dramatic difference between juvie and prison. Diana's third trip resulted in her spending her entire third decade at the unit where they were headed. That trip, she had been arrested for drugs, as usual. But while she was sitting in the back of the patrol car, she realized the handcuffs were not on right. The cops were still outside the car, but they left the doors open. That small mistake on their part gave her an idea. She got her hands free and for some stupid reason, thought it would be a good idea to steal the police car to get away. It wasn't.

The back door where she was sitting was not closed all the way. Once her hands were free, she inched her way out of the door. Being underweight because of her drug use made it easy to slither out unnoticed. Squatting on the pavement, her head twitched from right to left making sure no one was watching. One hand stayed on the side of the car for balance as she made her way slowly around the front of the car. Both officers were in the back talking on the radio and never noticed a thing. She finally reached the driver's door and jumped into the seat. *Dumb cops; who leaves keys in the ignition?* Twisting the keys, Diana pounded the gas and was off. It didn't take long for them to catch her and that stunt added an auto theft charge to the drug charge. The two charges together caused her to do ten years straight. Sitting in jail that night she began to realize who the dumb one was that afternoon. That was hard time, and you would've thought she'd learned her lesson, but this bus ride was proof she had not.

An hour later, the bus came to a stop and all the women began their time. Sadly, Diana was facing five years. Hopefully, she would make parole and release early. As usual, she would pass her time participating in any courses offered through the chapel or school.

At first it was like it was in the past, just participate to make time pass. But this time it was in one of those Bible studies that Diana got serious about her life. The volunteer who led the class really liked Diana, and they talked often about her ability to change. It was in one of those conversations that Diana decided it was time. This next time she got out, she would do anything and everything to keep from going back to prison. It was time to grow up and take responsibility for her life and do better.

Eighteen months later, Diana stood outside of central command in the center of the unit trembling. The day was here. Parole provided her with some pretty crappy clothes, but at least it was not the orange prison jumpsuit. After checking badges and clearances, the guard inside of central opened the gates. Diana was escorted to the exterior gate. As she walked out the gate to freedom, she was determined it would be her last time leaving prison. She had all her belongings in a mesh bag and fifty dollars to get a bus to her destination, the Samaritan House. Three hours later, she was sitting in the office of the home with Marty, the program director, filling out forms and learning all the rules.

Diana heard about the Samaritan House and knew it would be her best option. In the last twenty-five years, she had only spent a handful in the free world. And even then, she was high most of the time. She had much to learn. The best part was that Samaritan House had an incredible job-readiness program called Retake. She began with basic computer classes and then took more advanced courses. She loved all she was learning and discovered she was smart. She decided she should attend college and enrolled for the next fall semester.

One of the requirements at Samaritan House was to participate in restorative justice programming. They had a variety of different programs, some for victims, some for families of offenders, some for criminal justice professionals, and some for offenders themselves. Like everyone else, Diana was not excited about participating. But Trish, the executive director, insisted they take responsibility for all the harms done by the crimes they committed. Diana started with Letters from Home. Each month they were to write to a woman that was accepted into Samaritan House but was still incarcerated awaiting parole. Letters from Home was the one program most of the women liked. It felt good to encourage and help women like themselves.

She also volunteered for Giving Back. Each month the women living in the home would have a car wash or bake sale to raise money. That money was put into a victim compensation fund. From time to time, the victim advocate with the local police or sheriff's department would encounter someone elderly or disabled, who had been the victim of theft or burglary. Most of the time, the items stolen were televisions or something similar and the victim advocates could contact the Giving Back program and request funds to replace the stolen item. Diana really liked this program because she used to be the person stealing things. Replacing stolen items made her feel like she was doing something good.

The first time that Diana volunteered, the group went to meet with the victim advocate at the sheriff's department. Diana didn't mind working with the advocate, but deep down she hated cops. Most of them treated her like scum when they arrested her in the past. But she went anyway. Diana's volunteer group met a group of officers as they carried in a television that was going to an elderly woman who had been robbed. Diana recognized Deputy Jones because he arrested her on her last felony charge. He recognized her as well.

He walked over, stuck out his hand and said, "Well, hello, Diana. Good to see you. Good to see you doing so well."

A short sigh escaped from Diana's lips as she smiled back and shook his hand, "It is good to be on the right side this time. And can you believe, I am putting back a TV and not taking it?"

They both laughed. They all stood around and talked and visited until it was time to go. That was the first of many similar encounters that completely changed how Diana viewed people. She never thought she would see things in a different way, but she was changing. And it was good.

RESTORATIVE JUSTICE

Diana's story shows us the power of restorative justice—the fifth principle in this book. By being part of the program at the sheriff's department that replaced the stolen television, Diana gained insights into how her past behavior harmed others. Later in her story, you will hear how accountability for people she personally harmed became a turning point that repaired one of her relationships and changed Diana's life trajectory.

If you have participated in a restorative justice process, like circles, you realize that much can be accomplished through the power of the process in a short period of time. Even if you don't know how it happened, you are keenly aware of what happened. Before we get started, writings about restorative justice are often abstract and broad. We are going to try to make the chapter as concrete as possible because there are concrete structures and processes in restorative justice. However, why these processes create such rapid and significant change can be challenging to understand. For those who have not participated in restorative justice processes, you may find yourself asking, *Does that really work?* or *How could that happen?* Our hope is you will stay with us, push through, and explore how these elements and processes can be implemented in your business even if you don't fully know the why yet. We also hope this basic information about restorative justice and its impact will inspire you to learn more. Having even one person trained in restorative justice practices could have an incredible impact on your organization because restorative justice works.

What Is Restorative Justice?

"Restorative justice is a way of responding to conflict, misbehavior and crime that makes things as right as possible for all who were impacted."[1] Rather than focusing on the law or policy that was violated, restorative justice focuses on the people violated.[2] Restorative justice was originally used in the criminal justice system, but it has been applied to many different contexts, including business.[3]

Cheryl learned restorative justice through her experience as a volunteer mediator for the Victim Offender Mediation Dialogue (VOMD) program at the Texas Department of Criminal Justice. The program is part of the Victim Services Division. Cheryl began volunteering with VOMD in 2001 and has more than a thousand hours mediating between victims of violent crime and their offenders, who are in prison. It was the amazing transformations that Cheryl witnessed after a few short hours of the mediation that inspired her to explore the transferability of restorative justice to other settings.

The housing program Cheryl ran was considered a restorative justice organization. They did not use processes like VOMD, but they did implement each of the elements that make restorative justice work into the daily operations, philosophy, and culture. And when they did, the impact and transformation that occurred for the women they served was dramatic. When restorative justice is used outside the criminal justice system, it is called *restorative practice*. Throughout the chapter, we will talk about each concept in the context of restorative justice and also how businesses can use restorative practices to support their operations and their employees, including women with challenging pasts.

In Criminal Justice.   Restorative justice deviates from the mainstream system of justice currently in place in the United States. In the US criminal justice system, we operate with a retributive justice model. The model is rooted in the theory that punishment, when proportionally appropriate, is an acceptable and effective response to crime and injustice. In a retributive system, there are three questions asked: What laws have been broken? Who broke the law? and What is the penalty for breaking that law?

Alternatively, in restorative justice, we ask three different questions: Who has been harmed? What are their needs? and Whose obligation is it to meet those needs?[4] As you can see from these questions, the retributive system is perpetrator-focused and punishment-centric. In contrast, restorative justice is victim-focused and centered on restoration for those harmed.

There are many different restorative justice processes. The two most common are restorative justice circles and victim-offender dialogue (VOD). Throughout this chapter, we will focus on circles because they have great potential for integration into business practices. In the criminal justice system, circles are considered a form of facilitated dialogue and brings together stakeholders that will be impacted by the discussion. In circles, all participants have a say in all phases of the process. Circles can be used after a conviction and sentencing to give the victim and offender an opportunity for restoration from the harm done. Additionally, circles can be used to determine sentencing. Through consensus decision-making, the group participating in the circle—offender, victim, family, facilitator, possibly law enforcement, and when appropriate, members of the community—can determine the offender's sentence. All stakeholders have to agree, and the judge will accept the decision made in the circle.

During circles, stakeholders are seated in a circle with a facilitator to help guide the dialogue. At the beginning, the group sets norms together for the session based on the values of all involved. The facilitator starts the discussion with a question. Then a "talking piece" is passed to the person next to them. No one can talk without the talking piece, even the facilitator. No cross talk or interruptions are allowed.

The process is different from other discussions because everyone has an opportunity to respond to everything the facilitator poses to the group. For each pass or question, the talking piece will make its way around the entire circle. The process gives everyone an equal opportunity to contribute every time.

In Business. In business, like in criminal justice, restorative practices can be used to address conflict and harm. However, they may also help strengthen the entire organization, unify teams, and support individuals. Similar to the three questions asked in restorative justice, when implementing restorative practices, the business might ask: Who are our stakeholders? What are their needs? and How are we positioned to meet those needs?

There are two approaches for businesses to implement restorative practices. First, they can use restorative justice *processes* in the work setting. For example, circles have broad uses in business. Businesses use circles for strategic planning, team-building, facilitating difficult dialogues, revamping staff meetings, addressing conflict, and more. Each of these processes in business are more effective when everyone has an equal voice and when consensus can be reached. Restorative practices accomplish those goals.

Second, businesses can incorporate each *element* of restorative justice separately into their culture and operations like Cheryl did in her housing program. Our hope is businesses will both adopt individual elements of restorative justice and implement restorative justice processes.

Requirement for Restorative Justice and Practices

Fundamentally, restorative justice and practices are communication strategies that bring about transformation. A critical element of communication is active listening. Although we don't provide details about active listening here, we provide resources in the appendix that can be used to improve your active listening skills and enhance these elements of restorative justice. The five main elements of restorative justice—direct voice, stakeholder focus, safe place, value-based, and accountability—are required for this communication process to be effective. Communication is key in business, which is why the principles used in high-stakes dialogues between victims and offenders are effective for companies as well. In describing each of the five elements, we provide the element's application first in the criminal justice system (restorative justice) and then in business (restorative practices), especially for those employing women like Diana.

Stakeholder Focus.   A stakeholder includes all parties who have an interest in the decision made or particular issue. Even independent of restorative justice, stakeholder focus is gaining importance and attention in business.

In criminal justice: In restorative justice, stakeholders are identified by asking the question, Who has been impacted by this crime? In addition to the victim and offender, crimes can impact families, the community, law enforcement, or other secondary victims. In the restorative justice process, facilitators intentionally seek to identify all the stakeholders to determine if those voices are critical to the process. Often restorative justice circles are used to determine a sentence for a crime committed. The stakeholders include the victim, the perpetrator, and possible support persons for each. They could also include law enforcement and community members. The stakeholders then discuss the impact the crime has on each person and as a group determine the sentence.

In business: Many leaders are calling for a more stakeholder-oriented approach. As we discussed in the introduction, for so long, corporations have singularly focused on increasing shareholders' wealth—a concept referred to as *shareholder primacy.*[5] The restorative stakeholder approach shifts away from concern only for the impact on shareholders and more broadly considers the company's impact on all individuals or groups.[6]

Employees are key stakeholders in corporations. One study found employees often perceive other stakeholders receive more attention than they do. Further, the scholars found these beliefs are correlated with lower levels of employee commitment to the firm.[7] The scholars said,

> At their most basic level, the findings demonstrate that employees believe they get the smallest piece of the stakeholder pie. Because such perceptions are associated with lower commitment to the firm, companies must recognize that slighting employees relative to customers and shareholders can lead to attendance, retention, productivity and performance problems.[8]

Restorative practices are another tool for turning attention to employees as the critical stakeholders they are. Specific to women overcoming challenging pasts, they too would benefit from viewing employees as critical stakeholders. Viewing an individual as a whole person, and as a stakeholder, can dramatically improve an employee's work experience and, as scholars have noted, their productivity and performance.[9] Companies' awareness of the stakeholders in their employees' lives might consider offering flex schedules, on-site daycare, and paid leave for counseling appointments and fitness. Employers can consider what their stakeholders, with their input, value most in developing initiatives that treat employees as important stakeholders.

Direct Voice.   Direct voice gives each stakeholder an opportunity to speak about the issue. Their position may (as in consensus decision-making) or may not influence the outcomes, but they have an opportunity to directly provide input into the outcome or issues.

In criminal justice: Direct voice has several meanings in restorative justice:

1. Victims and offenders have an opportunity to talk to each other *directly*, with a mediator or facilitator. Victims get to say how the crime impacted them. They can share the full scope of harm done by sharing their story. The victim can also ask the offender questions to gain an understanding, such as *Why did this happen? What were the details? Do you know what you did?* Additionally, the offender directly speaks to the victim to provide insight for understanding or healing.

2. Victim's voices have power because the victim gets *direct* say in what they want to happen going forward and what needs to be done to repair the harm. Their ideas can be used to determine consequences.

Having a voice returns power to the victim.

The traditional criminal justice systems and society at large frequently minimize and, at times, dismiss the victim's experience and the harmful impact of violent crime on the victim. Through direct voice, victims tell their story. In retelling the story, victims can create meaning and begin to rebuild a former life. Without a direct voice and the ability to speak to the individual responsible for the harm, victims are left with only speculation and imagination.[10] And lack of understanding can be harmful and create an ongoing sense of victimization or harm.

Further, hearing directly from the victim allows the person responsible to understand the full impact of the harm done. Such understanding is rarely achieved in the traditional criminal justice system.

In business: Similarly, in a business context, direct voice:

1. Encourages employees to talk to each other *directly*, especially when conflict occurs or trust is broken. Such direct conversations could occur with or without a mediator or facilitator, depending on if the company is implementing restorative practice elements or processes. Going to the boss and hoping they will resolve the conflict erodes trust among the team,[11] creates an additional burden for the boss, and is not as effective in providing insight for understanding or healing.
2. Gives power to employees' voices, because they have *direct* say in what they want to happen going forward. This may be in the context of repairing harm but, hopefully, more often, this in setting the strategic direction of the company, team, or individual's trajectory. For example, restorative practices, such as circles, allow each participant to contribute to the strategic planning process. Through the structured process, every employee has an opportunity to provide input on each idea, challenge, or dream.

These restorative practices can reduce conflict and increase buy-in.

Initiatives to achieve direct voice can be large or small. Shannon was touring a facility for a large organization, and they had a board in the middle of the breakroom. Anyone in the company could write suggestions—large and small—on the board. Concerns on the board ranged from the breakroom being out of ketchup to serious suggestions for improving operations. Company leadership responded to every single comment. Shannon went back to her office and implemented the board immediately. A small adjustment like that can increase employees' opportunities for direct voice.

Specific to women overcomers' engagement in a business, most women are used to social service providers "telling" them what to do and how to access resources. Some companies would continue such a culture, but where women will have the greatest impact on the business and thrive most is in companies that encourage employees to have a direct voice. The shift from being told what to do and how to do it, to asking what they think and what needs to happen can create excitement and motivation. As seen in the stories in this book, women emerging from challenging lifestyles have a great deal to offer. Give them a direct voice by planning new projects or products and providing insight into day-to-day operations for improvement or efficiency. Creating opportunities for direct voice requires creating a safe place.

Safe Place. A safe place, whether tangible or conceptual, is an environment where stakeholders feel as comfortable as possible providing their input. The key components are the presence of structure, along with willingness, openness, respect, dignity, and an opportunity to be heard as described in this section.

In criminal justice: Creating a safe place is especially critical in a criminal justice context for victims of severe and violent crimes. For example, when considering taking a woman who has been sexually assaulted into a prison to sit six feet across the table from the man who assaulted her, the first and most basic need is the creation of a safe place. This is not to say the woman will feel completely safe. It is more to say she feels safe enough to enter that space.

Structure involves the specific processes, guidelines, and steps that govern restorative justice processes. We scratched the surface on the structure of circles in this chapter, but training is required to learn to effectively facilitate the restorative justice process.

Further, to create a safe place, all stakeholders must be willing to participate openly. The more willing the parties are, the more effective the outcomes. For victims to get additional information from the offender about the crime, to hear the offender's remorse, both parties need to be open to listening and speaking.

Additionally, dignity and respect are necessary for a safe place. Through respect, the space is void of interruptions, derogatory language, name-calling, and negative nonverbal communication. Similarly, dignity requires seeing the humanity in people, even in those we do not like or trust and those we deem enemies. Even those deemed the worst in society are someone's son, brother, sister, or mother.

Finally, the process relies on the opportunity to be heard. The opportunity for all stakeholders to be heard, which is often absent in traditional criminal justice, becomes a motivator to continue what can be a challenging process.

In business: Most companies recognize the value of safety for employees. But most safety procedures focus on physical safety of employees. How often do managers intentionally create an atmosphere of interpersonal safety among employees? When implementing restorative practices into business in any context it is important to create a safe place. In strategic planning, employees must feel safe to share their ideas. Team members must feel safe to begin to share values and goals in team-building. If restorative practices are used in staff meetings, employees must feel safe to share concerns with their supervisor present.

For businesses, structure often involves policy. However, restorative practice can provide additional structure for facilitating and encouraging direct discussions about any issues, even when it is challenging. As in the criminal justice system, employees must be willing, open, respectful, and treat each other with dignity.

The aspect of a safe place that may require the most intentionality for businesses is the opportunity to be heard. Unfortunately, not everyone in an organization feels safe speaking up. For example, the Society for Human Resource Management (SHRM) found 47 percent of Black human resource professionals do not feel they have a safe place for expressing their opinions about racial injustice at work. Though both White and Black employees agree race-based discussions could be uncomfortable, in contrast, only 28 percent of White HR professionals were uncomfortable discussing racial injustice in the workplace.[12] Without feeling safe, not everyone's voice will be heard. This study shows some of the most important voices on these challenging topics might be the most silenced in the workplace. Women also often have a harder time being heard in organizations. For example, even if women do feel comfortable speaking up, studies have shown they get interrupted more often.[13] Business could make significant progress in creating a safe place by adopting restorative practices. Doing so would benefit all stakeholders.

Specific to working with women overcomers, some have experienced extensive trauma, and they have felt silenced (without an opportunity to be heard). Many have lived in situations without dignity and respect. Companies will need to ensure their culture treats all stakeholders with dignity and respect before hiring women overcoming challenging pasts.

Value-Based. Values can be expressed as ideas or feelings about the worth of something. When individuals value something, they think that it is worth having, worth defending, worth seeking, or worth doing. Everyone has values. But people can be unaware of their values. Values, whether conscious or unconscious, are a standard by which people tend to judge others' behaviors, thoughts, and ideas. Values are critical in criminal justice and in business.

In criminal justice: Victims' and offenders' values influence restorative justice dialogue and are best identified prior to any interactions. Having previous insight into opposing values prior to dialogue can prepare both victims and offenders, especially when there are disparities in values. For example, often truth is an important value that victims bring to the process. Many need to know exactly what happened and why. Their hope is for offenders to be honest and tell the truth.

In business: Many companies recognize the importance of establishing values. Most organizations spend time crafting and sharing the values of the company with both employees and customers. However, companies must recognize that each of their employees has his or her own set of values. Values are at the root of many workplace conflicts.

Awareness of participants' values can maximize the positive benefits of restorative practices. For example, if an employee is hurt because pay is not equivalent, providing additional vacation time likely would not be sufficient means to address the hurt.

Women like Diana would also benefit from their employer understanding their values. For example, if they value sobriety, giving them time to attend a weekly Alcoholics Anonymous (AA) or Narcotics Anonymous (NA) meeting might make them a more committed employee. If employees value family, letting them leave early from time to time to make an important family event could have a significant impact on their performance. People recovering from poverty have been found to value relationships more than others because those relationships are necessary to survival.[14] This value in a work setting, particularly where team-building client relationships are required, is an asset. As an employer, take time to explore the values each person holds without prejudice or personal expectations.

Accountability: One of the significant components of restorative justice or restorative practices is the need for accountability.

In criminal justice: When one person or group harms another, it is imperative that the one who did the damage accepts responsibility before beginning the restorative process. In processes like VOD, if the offender does not take responsibility for the harm caused, then restorative justice cannot take place. It is easy to see how *other* people do or do not take responsibility for the harms they have done. However, we may be less aware or intentional about owning our own wrong acts.

As humans, our brains have developed some tools that allow us to avoid responsibility. In the original training manual for the VOMD program, these were called *common thinking errors*. The manual listed 120 thinking errors that can interfere with accountability in restorative justice, including making excuses, blaming others, or minimizing and justifying our actions. For example, someone blaming others in a criminal justice setting might say, "I only took it, because he told me to do it." The good news is that we can develop the ability to hear these thinking errors in ourselves and others. Redirecting or correcting thinking errors moves people toward greater accountability.

In business: Common thinking errors are prevalent in most offices. The telltale word to red flag common thinking errors is the word *but.* "*I know I hurt her, but. . . .*" Using the word *but* negates everything that came before it in a sentence. Begin to listen for those thinking errors and use moments in everyday conversations to practice helping people hear their words. And even better yet, start becoming aware of when you do it. When you use phrases to apologize like: "*but I was only trying to . . .*"; or "*it's just that . . .*"; or "*I only did that because . . .*"; you may be minimizing or making excuses.

Thinking errors with women like Diana can be common. What becomes important is how those thinking errors are addressed. The phrase *compassionate confrontations* was coined about the approach Cheryl took working with women. Cheryl was adept in recognizing thinking errors because of her experience working with offenders in the VOMD program. She also knew the value and power of addressing those thinking errors to allow women to move through any shame they were masking with thinking errors. She also knew the method of confrontation is important. Without trust and a form of respect or compassion, the confrontation may feel more like judgment.

In a work setting, two things typically can happen when individuals feel judged, either they shut down and walk away, or they lash out. Both reactions are not effective in building a healthy work environment. Managers need to explore how to build both effective relationships and trust to allow employees, including women with challenging pasts, to take personal responsibility for mistakes.

Personal responsibility can't be demanded, but it can be cultivated. We can force accountability through policies or laws, but we cannot demand that someone take personal responsibility. But managers and business owners can cultivate an atmosphere that allows employees to be honest when mistakes are made without retribution. Doing so keeps work relationships healthy and productive.

Creating Restorative Practices

The first step in creating opportunities to implement restorative practices in business is shifting to that restorative lens. As mentioned, businesses can implement each element separately as part of their culture and operations or they can incorporate restorative processes, like circles. The following questions could help companies determine where they could benefit most from restorative practices:

- Are meetings free from interruptions?
- Do employees feel they have a direct voice in to the operations, management, or culture?
- How does management constructively respond to feedback?
- Is harm addressed or ignored?
- Are employees at all levels given an opportunity to express concerns?
- Does the organization seek and give voice to allies willing to speak up when someone's voice is marginalized?
- Are all stakeholders considered?
- Is there space to explore values of employees that allows for understanding or building on shared values?
- Are employees and supervisors held accountable for harm done?
- Are managers trained in assisting employees in assuming greater accountability?

Organizations prepared to implement restorative justice have an opportunity to increase inclusiveness, mitigate harm, and make employees feel valued.

DIANA REBUILDS

The morning started out great. Trish had arranged meeting with some local business leaders seeking to understand how things worked at the home. Several of those present in the meeting hired women graduating from Samaritan House and were impressed with their work ethic. They were eager to know what was making such a difference. Trish asked Diana and several other women to participate in the meeting to provide the client's perspective.

Things had gone well until Diana made the comment, "I just wish my family, mainly my daughter Katy, would get the fact that I made a mistake."

Trish chimed in immediately, in front of everyone and corrected, "Diana, it was not a mistake. It was a crime. Buying and selling heroin is a crime, not a mistake."

Talk about embarrassing, Diana tried to hide her feelings and continued with her story. But it was the truth: it wasn't a mistake; it was a crime. Fortunately, everyone was gracious and commended her for all she was doing to make changes.

The meeting ended and after all the business leaders left, Diana and Trish locked up and headed back to the main house. As they walked across the parking lot, Diana tried to explain what she meant about making a mistake. Trish stopped and listened but she wasn't buying it. As they stood in the parking lot, Trish began to talk to Diana about taking responsibility for her past actions.

It made sense as Diana thought about it, but then Trish added, "I am pretty sure your daughter won't have anything to do with you because you refuse to take accountability for the harms you have done."

What a low blow. What a bitch. Who does she think she is all high and mighty? Diana's beet red face and arms locked straight by her side with her hands balled in fists was a clear indication to Trish that she just pushed a button. Diana trembled as anger bubbled from her gut, and by the time she felt it in her chest it was full-blown rage. Diana wanted to tell, no scream all her angry thoughts at Trish, but something stopped her. As she stood there swirling in emotions, it hit her hard. Trish was right. She didn't know what made her madder, the fact Trish made the comment or the fact she was right.

Trish looked at Diana and Trish's face and voice became so gentle. "Diana, you can do something about it. Take accountability and just think of one person you hurt that you can go to and repair the harm."

The tenderness of her voice was like the plug that was pulled allowing her rage to drain away. Upon hearing her words, Diana immediately thought of her sister, Carolyn. Diana and Katy lived with her the last time she got out of prison. And as usual back then, Diana was quickly back into her old ways and using. Needing money for drugs, she knew where Carolyn kept her emergency funds. Without a second thought, Diana waited until Carolyn left for work, and took four hundred dollars from the back of her closet. She knew that money was for her boys back-to-school shopping, but it didn't matter. The high was all she thought about.

Remembering that incident, Diana looked at Trish and said, "I know who. My sister, Carolyn. I stole from her the last time I lived there."

Trish started talking about how she could do something to make it right. She could go to her sister and repay her. Hearing those words, Diana's face turned white and the trembling returned. This time it was not rage but shame.

"I can't go there. I am too ashamed."

"Yes, you can. You are doing everything you should. There is no reason you can't go back to her and make this right, too."

Diana knew that was true, and two days later she and Trish left to visit Carolyn. Diana took four hundred dollars from the money she saved from working part-time. It was money she planned to use to buy a car, but that would have to wait. Trish set up the meeting with Carolyn by asking if they could visit. Trish would be there as support for the sisters. Carolyn agreed and now the three of them were sitting in the small living room of Carolyn's apartment.

Diana handed Carolyn the money and explained how sorry she was for all she put Carolyn through and for stealing the money. Carolyn started to cry and told Diana she couldn't take the money and that Diana should keep it to help her rebuild her life. Diana insisted and went on to explain, it was the least she could do. Diana continued saying she finally understood how much crap Carolyn put up with over the years because of Diana's addiction, including the fact she practically raised Katy. Finally, Carolyn agreed to take the money and grabbed Diana in a hug. It was a sweet moment, and they were about to leave when Diana heard a noise behind her.

She turned to see Katy. Diana couldn't believe her eyes. She had not seen Katy in three years. Here she stood as a young woman, so beautiful and tall.

"Mom, I was in the other room and heard everything. I am so proud of you for doing that."

Diana opened her arms and said, "I could really use a hug."

And with that Katy flew into Diana's arms. They froze in that position for minutes. Carolyn walked over and joined the family hug and all three held each other and wept. On the way back to the home, Diana explained to Trish, "I had hoped taking accountability for my actions would bring Katy back into my life."

Trish laughed and said, "But you didn't think it would take only a minute."

That day changed everything for Diana. She became unstoppable. As time went on, the expertise Diana learned at Retake and in college gave her courage to apply for a job at Stonebrook. Stonebrook had a major plant, manufacturing oilfield equipment. The plant housed both the manufacturing side of the business and the warehouse and distribution side. Diana applied for a job as an administrative assistant to the head of the warehouse department. Fortunately, there was no box on the application asking about criminal history.

Nervous didn't even come close to how Diana felt that morning before her interview. At one point in the interview, Diana's lips quivered. She quickly clamped her bottom lip between her teeth to make it stop. She prayed the interviewer missed her attempt to calm shaky lips. An hour later, the interview ended, and Diana was told they would follow up later in the week.

Exactly one week later, Diana was filling out forms in the HR department for her new position as administrative assistant to Mike Evans. Never in a million years had Diana dreamed she could or would work in an office. All her past jobs had been labor-intensive and physically demanding like 70 percent of the jobs typically filled at Stonebrook. This time she would be in administration.

The HR specialist working with Diana explained that during their background check they discovered her felony convictions. Typically, they were hesitant to hire individuals with backgrounds like hers on the administrative side, but Mike was insistent in giving Diana a chance. He said that he saw something in Diana and admired the way she spoke and carried herself despite her past. Diana was shocked to hear that because she thought she acted like a frightened kitten during the interview. But either way, she was thrilled to get the job. Not only was it a real job in a real office, but the money she was going to make was also triple any other job she ever had. It wouldn't be long with this salary to earn enough money to move from Samaritan House to her own apartment.

WHY RESTORATIVE JUSTICE WORKS

All the research in the world cannot capture the depth of restorative justice's effectiveness. The second mediation Cheryl did was with a woman whose only child was murdered. Ten years after the crime, she met face-to-face with the man who killed her son. The mediation lasted two hours. The following week, Cheryl checked in with the mother and asked her how she was feeling since the mediation. Her response was powerful. The mother went on to say, "It's hard to explain. It's like for the last ten years there has been this boulder on my chest, slowly crushing the life out of me, slowly crushing the breath out of me. And now it is gone. Now I can breathe again. Now I can live again." Let the impact of that sink in. In just two short hours, this mother went from slowly suffocating to being able to breathe again, to live again.

The statement made by the victim describes an abstract reality. Explaining life and death is complex and challenging. But that abstract reality emerged because of a tangible practical process of VOMD. A practical process that works in companies as well.

Cheryl worked with an organization that was frustrated by their unproductive efforts at strategic planning. She facilitated a circle for the team. With each pass around the circle, conflicting ideas and preexisting frustrations emerged. Because the stakeholders guided the focus of a circle, Cheryl guided them through the conflict. At times, the conversation got more heated, until the group uncovered the root of the conflict. In one round, one participant made a comment acknowledging the conflict but went on to say how much respect she had for each person in the group. Her comments shifted the entire dialogue.

The following time around the circle, the participants shared the strengths they saw in each other. The conflict was quickly resolved, and strategic planning resumed but now with productive outcomes. Two hours later, the circle concluded with tangible next steps for the organization. The atmosphere in the room was vibrant. What had not been accomplished in several traditional strategic planning meetings was accomplished in one 2-hour circle. As a bonus, they had a renewed commitment to each other and the company.

One participant shifted the focus from an issue creating conflict to the dignity of each person present. This type of shift is common in circles, and it is exactly why they are so powerful. But what happened was not magical or abstract. It happened because of a specific and proven process. There was structure in place, a process in place, and because of that participants felt safe to respond on a more intimate level. The facilitator trusted the process and the results were exactly what the group both wanted in strategic planning and needed in conflict resolution.

Restorative justice works because it is built on connecting to the humanity inherent in each person. In the middle of our busy lives we often forget to focus on the person or people we interact with daily. In the workplace, bottom lines and efficiency are all important, but in their pursuit, we must not forget to see the faces that are tasked with making each of those a reality.

> *Restorative justice works because it is built on connecting to the humanity inherent in each person.*

OWNING IT

Diana worked hard those first few years at Stonebrook. One of the favorite parts of her job was that each year the team in her department attended the annual Oilfield Equipment and Materials Conference. She loved the seminars on all the new innovations and systems. But this morning, she was sitting in Ted Madison's seminar. Ted was a colleague in her department, and she attended his session to show support, even though she had no interest in his topic of how to spot and hire the most productive employees.

At one point in his seminar, he commented, "If at all possible, avoid hiring individuals with felony convictions in the administrative side of the business." He went on to explain that it was common to hire those with felonies in the more labor-intensive types of jobs. Then he proceeded to talk about how the formerly incarcerated came with major issues and barriers. He incorrectly explained they were not eligible for government housing when they got out, making them unstable as employees as they moved around. He incorrectly said they were not eligible for financial aid to attend college so they would be limited in their educational background.

Diana could not believe what she was hearing. Where did he get his information? She knew firsthand that most of that was not true. She knew it wasn't because she attended college with a Pell grant. And when she left Samaritan House, she became eligible for a second step home that was funded by Housing and Urban Development (HUD). She lived there for the first two years she worked at Stonebrook and as she finished up her degree. After the seminar, she tried to get to Ted to ask where he got his incorrect information, but the line of people asking questions was longer than she desired to wait. She could catch up with him later.

Diana never found Ted at the convention but ran into him a week later at work. She told him she had attended his seminar and enjoyed most of it. She went on to say that some if his information was not correct.

Ted smirked at the comment, "Oh really. And what would that be?"

Few people at Stonebrook knew of her background and Ted certainly did not. Diana explained that formerly incarcerated and individuals with felonies could live in government housing and were eligible for government financial aid. She did not share she knew from experience.

Again, Ted smirked and, in a most condescending tone, said, "Well, I don't know where you get your information, but I have done extensive research. My doctoral dissertation was on the barriers ex-offenders face that impacts the workplace."

Diana fumed. At this point she explained she had been formerly incarcerated in another state and lived in government housing and attended college on government-assisted financial aid. Ted rolled his eyes.

Titling his head to one side he said, "You do realize that different states have different rules about how to use government funds. That may be what you experienced in that state, but it is not the case here in New York. Now if you excuse me, I have better things to do than talk about things you don't understand."

Diana fumed to her desk. *Who did he think he was? How dare he talk to her like that.* She knew what she was talking about. He was the idiot. She opened her laptop and within five minutes had compiled a list of HUD-funded housing projects that housed formerly incarcerated people in New York. She fired that information to Ted in an e-mail. She waited for an apology that never came. The next time she saw Ted, he completely ignored her. Sadly, this was not the first time Diana encountered ignorance when it came to those with a past. And even more sadly, she was used to it.

A part of her work was to monitor and increase sales. She was also responsible for compiling the monthly sales reports for management. Each month, she had to manually enter the last few contracts for the month, while accounting caught up. Once she finished entering the data for November, she noticed they experienced a spike in sales. When she took the report to Mike for his meeting with management, she showed him the increase. During a previous conversation, Diana mentioned the new software system she learned about at the annual conference. The unexpected revenue from last month was almost exactly what they needed to purchase the software. The software was touted to increase sales at least 10 percent, with a hopeful promise of up to 20 percent. Mike liked the idea and presented it to his team. After follow-up research, management agreed to purchase the software. After only one month of operating the new system, efficiency was up 18 percent. If that was the increase in the first few weeks of learning curves, it was exciting to watch to see how it could continue.

At the end of the year, Diana was compiling the final sales reports from accounting. The final numbers were too low. November was off. She spent the next four hours scouring over every detail in every column on her spreadsheets and accounting reports. She finally found the problem.

Diana messed up. When she manually entered the last few contracts for her preliminary report, she made a major mistake. Instead of entering $260,000, she accidentally transposed the two and the six so the numbers showed as $620,000. That was a $400,000 mistake. Diana swallowed hard to keep from losing the contents of her lunch. This was bad. This was very bad. She suggested the purchase of the new system based on a surplus that did not exist—a surplus that Diana created with an error. Her first thought was to leave the numbers and hope no one noticed. Or she could blame it on the accounting department. As her thoughts twisted fearing that she might be about to lose her job, she remembered the day in the parking lot, when Trish said, "I am pretty sure your daughter won't have anything to do with you because you refuse to take accountability for the harms you have done." *Accountability*. She knew what she needed to do. This was her fault and she had to own it now.

Diana walked to Mike's office. Lightly knocking on the door, Diana asked if they could talk. Mike invited Diana to sit. Diana swallowed, lowered her eyes, and began to explain what she had done. He was shocked.

"Oh my gosh. This is bad," Mike said softly.

"I know. I am so sorry. I cannot believe I did something this stupid. Do you need my resignation?" Diana replied.

Mike cocked his head and frowned, "Are you kidding? You made a mistake, but you are one of the best employees in this department."

With that Diana fought back tears. The two of them spent the next hour discussing what to do and how to pass on the information to the rest of management. The next day, they all sat in a meeting. Diana was terrified when she walked in the room, but she had to explain what happened. Of course, everyone was unhappy about such a huge mistake. The team discussed adjustments to be made to rectify the issue. Multiple times, Diana apologized. At the beginning the team acknowledged and accepted her regrets. After the fourth or fifth apology, another manager, Ken Sutherland, told her she need not apologize anymore. He said it was clear this was a mistake, and he was sure it would never happen again. The bright side to all this was the purchase of the system seemed to be working.

That system was Diana's suggestion. She had compiled the research Mike took to that original meeting. When she first heard about the software at the conference, she knew their current capacities and knew this had great potential. Her insight was spot on. As they looked at the numbers, Ken suggested this might be a serendipitous mistake. They would not have approved that system if the funds were not available. But if the early projections just continued, they would cover this cost of this mistake in the next two quarters and then go on to continue to increase efficiency and revenue.

As the meeting ended, the CEO Joseph Graves pulled Diana aside, "I hear you are the one who caught this mistake and reported it to Mike."

"Yes, I did. I had to."

Joseph stuck out his hand and grabbed Diana's, "We rarely see that kind of accountability and integrity these days. This is why you are so valuable to Stonebrook."

Diana was floored. She could not believe all that transpired. When she first found her mistake, she was sure it would cost her job. It had not, and now, the CEO was telling her she was valuable to Stonebrook. But then she remembered the day with Carolyn and how quickly an ugly situation turned around by simply doing the right thing and making things right.

She went back to her desk and thought back to that day in the parking lot with Trish. Diana remembered the rage and shame she felt that morning, but she also remembered the joy and freedom that came two days later when she owned her crap and held Katy for the first time in three years. That day set her on a path of integrity one would never imagine could be a reality for a former heroin addict much less a five-time felon. But it was true. Diana had integrity. She was a valued employee making a good living.

She leaned back on her leather chair and giggled to herself, "Go figure, who'd a thunk. But yes, this is my life!"

6

THERE'S THE DOOR

Partnerships

"You know what? There's the door. Why don't you save us all a lot of time and just leave now and go stick a needle in your arm?" Janet said as Maria looked at her in shock.

While Maria just sat with her mouth open, Janet continued, "You know the rules here. Don't pretend you don't. If you don't want to follow them, just save us all the time and go on out and use. I am not playing this game."

Maria's mind started racing. *I don't have anywhere to go. I really wanted to make it this time. I can't believe she just said that to me.*

As much as Maria wanted to be mad and bolt out the door, she also wanted a new life. She was tired. She was back at House of Grace for the second time. She just got out of prison for the sixth time. If she had listened to Janet the last time she was here, she would have never gone to prison that last time. No, she was going to do things different.

"Dang Janet, that's harsh. But you're right. I know the rules. I really don't want to leave. I promise I will do right."

Janet just stood there looking at her for what seemed like an eternity. Finally, she agreed to let Maria stay and turned and left the office. Maria let out a huge sigh. She was determined to make it this time. She would use every resource she had to make it. Maria went back to the main house. She had chores to do, and she was so tired. Even though she had been out of prison for three days, the tension from always being on guard had not left her muscles. As soon as it was dark, she headed upstairs. She hoped as soon as she hit the pillow, she would be asleep. Her eyes were heavy and wouldn't stay open, but her mind was still racing and wouldn't shut down.

Maria's first time at House of Grace was two years ago. She worked the program but really didn't *work* the program. Janet, the executive director of House of Grace, said she saw something in Maria. Maria liked that and was sure she could use that insight to get things others didn't get. Maria took advantage of classes they offered in their job-readiness program. She worked her way through each course.

The first course she took was Food for Futures. Participants learned all about working in the food industry, and restaurants in particular. House of Grace was in partnership with a local restaurant, the Green Horse Bistro. Women in Food for Futures learned all aspects of working at Green Horse and were paid as they trained. The most important thing Maria learned in that course was that she really didn't want a career in the food industry.

The next class she took was on entrepreneurship. She loved that class. They worked with a group of local business leaders to develop ideas for new businesses. Maria had so many good ideas. She was considering launching her own business when Janet asked her if she would be willing to work for Grace part-time to oversee the job-readiness courses. Because she wasn't 100 percent convinced she was ready to launch a business, she jumped on the opportunity. Part of her job was to take participants to job interviews upon graduation. House of Grace provided a vehicle for participants and because Maria was responsible for getting residents to job interviews, she had keys to the Malibu.

Everything was going along fine until an old friend from her past moved to the House of Grace. As soon as Maria saw Serena, she felt an uneasy feeling in her gut. Serena had been her dope buddy. They got high together all the time before Maria decided to stop. Of course, Serena was delighted to see Maria and rushed up and grabbed and hugged her.

"Girl, it is great to see a familiar face," Serena said.

The two sat and talked for the next thirty minutes catching up. Serena was referred to House of Grace by her probation officer. She was arrested a few months before for possession. After sitting in county jail, she was finally sentenced to three years' probation with the condition she go to House of Grace upon release. Serena told Maria she would go anywhere if it meant she could get out of county. She asked Maria if she had any weed. Maria assured her she did not and explained she was serious about her recovery.

Serena rolled her eyes and said, "Hmph, we'll see."

For the next two weeks, Serena and Maria were inseparable. Serena was sneaking out and getting high, but Maria never joined her. Maria wasn't going to use, but she did enjoy hanging out with Serena. Amy, the house mom, didn't trust Serena. She was pretty sure she was playing games. Amy warned Maria to be careful around Serena. So did Janet. Did they think she was stupid? She wasn't using and didn't plan to use. They were both right about Serena, though, but Maria wasn't going to snitch. If only she had listened.

One day, Serena convinced Maria to take her to an old friend's house. Maria reluctantly agreed and grabbed the keys to the Malibu. Serena told her to run by Capital Liquor to pick up some vodka and 4 six-packs of Seagram's Strawberry Daiquiri Escapes. Maria could feel her resolve slowly leaving her body as she sat in the car while Serena was inside. It was like someone pulled a plug in her toe and it was draining away. Serena returned with an armload of alcohol and a huge grin. Maria asked her where she got the money.

Serena grinned even bigger and said, "I guess Amy is not so smart leaving the House of Grace debit card on her desk."

Oh, this was not going to be good. For a split second, Maria thought about snatching the card, kicking Serena out and going home. But instead, she drove to the friend's house and went inside. That binge went on for five days and unfortunately was not limited to that first liquor run. Maria knew the pin number on the card because she was always with Amy when she did the grocery shopping. It was easy to see the pin code she punched in. Every time they hit the liquor store, they also hit the cash back option to buy dope. Maria knew it wouldn't be long before Amy or Janet figured out they were using the card and close it, but until then, Maria was going to party. And party they did, until she saw the red lights in the rearview mirror of the Malibu on their latest liquor run.

Maria pulled over and got ready to act dumb. But the cop pulled a gun and told her to get out of the car with her hands up. *What the hell? What's going on?* Now, Maria was freaking out. Both she and Serena were so high it took them a few minutes to process that they should get out of the car. After the last loud shout from the police, Maria opened the door and stepped out. Immediately she was on the ground with her hands behind her back. As they pulled her up, she asked what was happening, trying to play dumb. But the cops weren't having it and told her she was under arrest for auto theft.

That night was two years ago, and Maria remembered it like it was yesterday. She remembered laying on the metal bed in the county jail. She had just been arrested for theft from the debit card, possession of heroin, and auto theft. Her body felt like it was going to explode from coming down hard. How could she have been so stupid? She thought she had manipulated Janet enough that she wouldn't have her arrested. She was wrong. After a plea deal, Maria was sentenced to five years and went back to the Texas Department of Corrections (TDC).

When Maria got to TDC she was determined this would be her last time. She signed up for every class she could take. One course was a restorative justice program. She remembered all the restorative justice programs at House of Grace and knew it would be good. She also started going to every NA and AA meeting they offered. When she got to Step 8 her sponsor asked if she should add Janet and Amy to her list of people to make amends.

Maria felt like she had been slapped and said, "Me? Make amends to them? I am in prison because of them!"

Maria hated them for turning her in. Sure, she had the car, but she always planned to return it. And it was Serena who stole the card not her. How could her sponsor even suggest such a thing?

She was about to go on and explain all of that when her sponsor said, "Oh yeah, that's right. They gave you the car and debit card and told you to go get high and break the law. Of course, silly me. You are here because of them."

Maria wanted to get angry, but she knew that was true. As much as she didn't want to do it, she knew she needed to write to Amy and

Janet to make amends. The letters went out that afternoon. What was shocking to Maria were the two letters that came back two weeks later. Both women wrote and told her they forgave her and still loved her. Even more shocking, they said she could come home when she was serious and ready to change. Maria sat on her bunk trying not to cry. It didn't work.

Now here she was back out of prison, back at House of Grace, realizing she almost blew her second chance. She was determined that there was no way that would happen. She lay there telling herself, *You can do this, Maria. You can do this,* over and over until she drifted off to sleep.

THREE-POINT PARTNERSHIPS

As you will see throughout Maria's story, and as you have seen throughout the other five women's stories in this book, partnerships are necessary to create the best-case scenario to engage women from marginalized pasts into a successful business setting. The most effective partnerships involve a triangle with three participants. The three points of the triangle include—businesses, nonprofit organizations, and the women themselves.

In the introduction, we talked about the importance of businesses and nonprofit organizations coming together to solve the big problems in the world. We discussed the United Nations Sustainable Development Goals (SDGs). The significant challenges captured in the SDGs—poverty, hunger, gender equality, education for all, health, sanitation, climate, and so on—will not be addressed by government, nonprofit, or business alone. We will only succeed together. Each point in the three-point partnership brings significant value based on their strengths, expertise, experiences, and resources.

What Are Businesses' Roles in the Partnership?

The most impactful role businesses can play in the partnership is hiring women like Maria, working hard to overcome difficult pasts. Employing women overcomers in companies that implement the principles in this book will have a significant impact on the women, their families, communities, and the business. Investing in women becomes exponential as women, in turn, invest in their families.

Investing in women becomes exponential as women, in turn, invest in their families.

Further, the expertise business professionals have is not typically found in nonprofit work. Business professionals can help nonprofit organizations develop more sustainable solutions to the problems they are trying to address. Historically, nonprofit organizations have relied on donations to provide goods or services to those they serve. Donations are not always sustainable. More and more nonprofit organizations are looking to social enterprises, which is basically a business within the nonprofit that generates revenue, to fund their mission. Business professionals' expertise could provide extensive value to nonprofit organizations working to start a social enterprise. Plenty of nonprofit organizations are willing, but few have the expertise to get started. Business professionals could provide consulting services on business operations, accounting or bookkeeping, founding a business, and marketing. We have provided examples throughout this book of social enterprises, such as the Dream Center in chapter 3 and as you will see later in this chapter.

A business would benefit most from supporting a social enterprise aligned with their mission or strategic goals. For example, if the company's mission is to provide high-quality products to their customer, then a partnership with a nonprofit that has a social enterprise making high-quality, locally sourced products would be advantageous.

Many companies would benefit from increased economic development within the community because the community's spending power would increase. In those cases, companies could invest time and resources in overcomers' entrepreneurial efforts, like in several chapters in this book. Again, investing in entrepreneurial efforts aligned with the company's mission will likely have the greatest impact. For example, companies could look for nonprofits with social enterprises that could serve as suppliers. The partnership could almost work as an integrated supply chain, where the nonprofit makes something the company needs. We have seen organizations outsource different projects to the nonprofit organization in the partnership.

The partnership should be sustainable and beneficial for all parties. For example, if you operate a home goods store, then a partnership with a nonprofit that makes candles would be perfectly reasonable. However, if you operate an equipment company that partnership might be philanthropic but likely not strategic. Of course, individuals could invest in overcomers' entrepreneurial efforts for philanthropic reasons or investment purposes, depending on the arrangements made among the nonprofit, the entrepreneur, and the investors.

Businesses could encourage their employees to serve as mentors to emerging entrepreneurs like the women in this book. Their involvement could look much like the business professionals' engagement in chapter 3 with the LRT, who make another appearance later in this chapter. Such business professionals could review business plans, screen pitches for potential loans, and coach the entrepreneurs. These opportunities require engagement with the business, a nonprofit organization, and women. Finally, businesses can leverage their connection to create greater opportunities and increase access to resources for both the nonprofit and the women they serve.

What Are Nonprofit Organizations' Roles in the Partnership?

Nonprofit organizations have expertise in providing services to women from varied difficult backgrounds. The care provided must be comprehensive, including housing, counseling, life skills training, and drug rehabilitation, to name a few. Providing these services is not within the scope of a business's responsibilities or expertise. However, many nonprofit organizations are equipped to assess women's specific needs and to provide services to meet those needs, either through internal services or by outsourcing such services within their network. The nonprofit organization and not the business will know if the individuals served are getting the support they need. In fact, to ensure success, we would not recommend businesses hire women who have recently faced these challenges without some form of vetting process by the nonprofit.

Some nonprofit organizations also have job-training programs that meet the women's specific needs and are appropriate for their current skill sets. Businesses can greatly benefit from partnering with nonprofit organizations with effective job-training programs. Within a formal partnership, the nonprofit could provide training that specifically prepares women for jobs available in different industries and with specific businesses.

When the nonprofit organization provides basic job training, they can also screen potential hires. They have extensive experience in working with women seeking a better life. Although they could not predict with 100 percent accuracy, they can assess a potential hire's readiness for a job, skill sets, work ethic, and commitment to succeed. Nonprofit organizations that can provide talent to companies build a reputation in the community, if companies know that they can go there to find qualified hires with a strong work ethic. Such an arrangement could be particularly beneficial in helping companies who struggle to meet their human capital needs (i.e., with a limited pool, high turnover, etc.) to develop an employment pipeline.

Finally, nonprofit organizations could develop training for supervisors within the companies who are going to oversee women overcomers. The nonprofit provides insight on working with the population as well as principles similar to those covered in this book. This training ensures supervisors are ready to manage the new hires seeking a better life. Businesses and nonprofits will experience the greatest success when their partnership involves significant engagement with the women.

What Are Survivors' or Overcomers' Roles in the Partnership?

In chapter 2, we emphasized the importance of survivor leadership. Survivor leadership included engaging women in their own recovery and in the operations of the nonprofit providing them support. Related to the business partnership, women overcoming challenging pasts should be engaged in every aspect of the process of transitioning from the services provided by the organization to gainful employment. One of the significant challenges women in Shannon's study faced was finding legally acceptable employment.

For the first jobs after exiting the sex trade, the women in the study struggled to find appealing work at a decent wage. One participant said, "I got a job as a fry cook. Oh, my gosh, I hated it. I worked there for three weeks and I thought, 'why me?'"[1] Another said, "My first job was just awful. Rolling tamales, like two or three hundred a night. And then I was busting my ass all night for fifty bucks." The issue was they knew an "easier way to get money." They had "numbers memorized," meaning they could call a John to pay them for sex, instead of being a fry cook and rolling tamales. One of the women who Cheryl worked with said to her, "I got sober for this?" about a job she hated.

Involving women in the partnership can help then find jobs that will be more appealing when first exiting those other livelihoods. At a minimum, it can help them find jobs that will move them closer to their goals. Let's look at an example of what happens when a partnership does not give equal standing to women and only focuses on the businesses and a nonprofit organization. In this example, let's assume a nonprofit organization has established partnerships with several local businesses. All of the businesses are restaurants.

So, most of the women go to work in a restaurant as their first job, while receiving support from the organization. However, many of the women don't have any interest in working in food services long term. Such a partnership is not well aligned to support all women. By involving the women in the partnership, the women can work with the nonprofit to find partnerships with businesses in industries that are more appealing to them. Then women can find work that will move them in the direction of their longer-term interests.

The nonprofit organization and the business will benefit from partnering with the women. For the nonprofit, women can run a social enterprise (remember chapter 2, which covered immediate leadership opportunities, and chapter 4, which covered translation factor). With the right scaffolding, the women took on responsibility and translated the skills they already had into benefiting the organization. In chapter 2, engaging women as leaders improved the programming the organization offered. Women can develop and teach programming for others based on what they see as the need. The women receiving services have much more expertise in their own experiences than nonsurvivor organization leaders. Finally, women overcomers can serve on the board of directors of nonprofit organizations to guide the organization's strategic direction in a way that best serves the population.

A central theme of this book has been that companies can benefit from hiring women who have overcome significant challenges. Companies may be tempted to view hiring such women as a philanthropic strategy. Of course, it would benefit the women hired, but the true benefit will be with the company. By implementing the principles in this book, companies can effectively incorporate a diverse perspective into their organization by hiring women who have had such unique experiences. Their perseverance and tenacity alone will benefit a company. Then these principles will let companies further benefit from the women's' resourcefulness, resilience, ability to hustle (i.e., work ethic and marketing strategies), and to motivate others.[2]

Having other women who have started the process of transformation and are further along in the pipeline can improve the onboarding and transition process for new hires. As managers, women overcomers bolster the pipeline by screening and training new employees. They work to ensure policies and practices are nonexploitative and prevent revictimization. For the partnership to reach its full potential, all three points of the partnership need to have a role.

Requirements of Three-Point Partnerships

Several requirements of a three-point partnership will help ensure the partnership makes a significant impact. First, each point in the partnership should be pursuing sustainable solutions—meaning to create something or an impact that can be maintained. We do not specifically mean environmentally sustainable solutions. Such solutions could be the focus, depending on the mission of the organizations involved. However, for most partnerships, the focus on sustainability will be on profit and people. Meaning, we must ask, "Are these financially sustainable solutions that positively impact stakeholders?" The business will typically have greater strengths in the profit area, and the nonprofit will typically have greater strengths related to people, particularly those they serve. Both are important.

Nonprofit organizations have not always been challenged to create sustainable solutions. For example, teaching women to make and sell jewelry typically will not provide them sufficient income or skills they can use to gain appealing employment with a reasonable wage. We offend organizations that run social enterprises with unsustainable products or training from time to time when we say that, but the message is important enough that it needs to be said anyway. Organizations must provide women with skills that will translate into legitimate employment that pays a decent wage.

Similarly, Shannon created a course for college students called "Business Solutions to Social Problems." The course was designed to inspire business students to use business expertise to address social issues. As we stated before, most business courses focus on increasing shareholders' wealth as the purpose of business. The students in this course were surprised and inspired by the idea that their business expertise could be used to create sustainable solutions to the world's biggest challenges.[3] Many business professionals would love to know their expertise could be used toward solving social problems. However, someone in a nonprofit organization might have to let the business professional know the nonprofit needs that expertise.

Next, for a successful partnership, all points must be balanced in their commitment, with each participant contributing what they do best. No partner can be too busy or too under-resourced to commit what is needed for success. This is most challenging for business professionals, for whom the partnership will likely not be their primary role. However, setting clear expectations about the time commitment up front will help increase success rates.

The Food for Futures project mentioned in Maria's story is a beautiful example of all three partnerships bringing equal commitment to the table. The story is modeled after a partnership Cheryl built with a local restaurant. Business leaders worked with the women to draft the business plan to run the restaurant. One leader on the business team knew the partnership would require a formal ownership agreement. The business leader contacted his personal business attorney and asked if the attorney would be willing to prepare the document and he gladly agreed. The women in the nonprofit researched and wrote all the curriculum that accompanied the training program. They also ran the day-to-day operations of the restaurant. The nonprofit was a co-owner of the local restaurant and did all the administrative activities like payroll, accounts receivable, and filing reports. The partnership was the epitome of mutually beneficial.

Each partner is unique but valuable, and the partnership will not work without balanced input from each point of the partnership.

Each participant's contribution must be valued equally. Non-profit leaders can get intimidated by business professionals in these partnerships if care is not taken. Considering chapter 5 and restorative justice principles, each participant must have a direct voice, that is, treated with respect and dignity, and each participant must listen actively. Each partner is unique but valuable, and the partnership will not work without balanced input from each point of the partnership.

Creating Three-Point Partnerships

When all three points in the partnership work together, effective impact grows significantly. The following questions could help companies consider the best partners and the best structure for a three-point partnership to accomplish a shared mission:

- Are we prepared to give an equal voice to all members of the partnership?
- Does our company have enough respect for women with difficult backgrounds to give them direct voice in the company's operations and the direction of the partnership?
- Is our company willing to commit to human and financial resources to the partnership?
- Do we have managers who are already trained or committed to becoming trained to work with women overcoming marginalized pasts?
- What local nonprofit organizations in the area meet the following criteria? The nonprofit:
  - Offers (or is interested in offering) sustainable solutions to addressing women's economic development.

- Provides comprehensive services to women with challenging pasts—counseling, legal advice, drug rehabilitation, housing, family reunification, and so forth.
  - Involves women they serve in their recovery.
- Do we respect the nonprofit organization and their mission enough to:
  - Work closely with them to achieve a goal, and
  - Value their input in the process?
- Have members of our company bought-in to the nonprofit's mission?

Working together allows everyone to focus on what they do well and contribute the best of their expertise.

SURPRISE ENCOUNTERS

Maria knew from her first time at House of Grace that she was smart. She decided to enroll in college to pursue a degree in psychology. Her first semester was brutal; she had to take remedial courses just to get to the basics. But she knew she had it in her and she plugged away. Each semester the classes got easier. Her days were filled with classes, working part-time, and attending NA meetings. She loved her NA community, and she quickly became a leader. She was elected the local representative to the region. It was at one of the annual state NA meetings that Maria saw James. She could not believe her eyes. James was alive. The last she heard he had overdosed and died. When he saw Maria, his eyes lit up.

He quickly crossed the room and said, "Hey wifey. Damn. You look great."

Maria couldn't believe her eyes but eventually smiled and said, "You don't look too shabby either hubby."

Maria and James were married about ten years previously. It began more as a way for Maria to have protection when she was in her hard-core drug days. He looked out for her and she, well, in her own way she looked out for him. Somewhere along the way though, Maria realized she really loved James. But in her typical Maria style she was

arrested, and she got word while in prison that James died of an over-
dose. Maria cried for days knowing she would never see him again.
But here he was standing right in front of her.

Finally, she slugged him in the arm and said, "Dude, I heard you
were dead."

James told her that he did die. He was with friends, and they
thought he had stopped breathing so they drove him to the ER and
left him on the sidewalk. He was still alive when the ER nurse found
him, but he crashed shortly after. He was told he coded three times.
He was in the hospital for three days. The day before he was to be
released, a social worker came in to talk about exit plans and asked if
he ever considered rehab.

James knew he had to give it a shot. Unfortunately, the only bed
open was in Amarillo—ten hours away. James's closeness to death
was enough for him to say yes. It turned out to be the best thing for
him. He stayed in rehab for six months and then moved to a sober
living house. He took seriously the recovery adage, "new playground,
new friends" and never reached out to anyone from his past. It had
worked. Here he was seven years later still sober.

They spent the next three days catching up. They both knew the
old spark was there, but James was hesitant to move on his feelings.
They lived so far apart. Could they really make a long-distance relationship work? When the conference ended, they agreed they would
not divorce and see if the distance thing could work. Six months later,
Maria transferred to a university in Amarillo, and she and James were
truly husband and wife for the first time.

James had a great job in the IT field, so when Maria graduated with
her bachelor's degree in business, he encouraged her to continue her
education. Maria was working part-time for Safe Harbor, a nonprofit
that provided counseling services to the most at risk, with payment
options on a sliding scale based on income. Most of their clients were
women and men with backgrounds like hers. She started there as a
receptionist, but her hope was one day to become a staff counselor.
And to make that a reality, she decided to enroll in graduate school
and pursue a master's degree in counseling. Two years later, she was
walking across the stage again—this time to be hooded. James sat on
the front row beaming. He was so proud of her. Seeing him in tears

as she crossed the stage made Maria's heart just burst with love. They had a good life.

Getting her degree was the first step. The bigger step would be to become a licensed professional counselor. Most states do not provide a license to individuals with felonies, and Maria had multiple. Fortunately, it was an option for her in Texas, but she was warned it was rare that the licensing board approved anyone with a felony, even more so someone with multiple. But that didn't faze Maria. She spent a full year working with the licensing board, meeting all requirements to be considered. The final step was an in-person interview. Maria showed up to that interview dressed in the most middle-of-the-road clothing she could find. The interview lasted more than an hour, and the board told Maria how impressed they were with all she had done to prepare and all she did to overcome. The meeting ended with them explaining she should receive word within a few weeks. Two weeks later she sat across from James at their small dining room table. They both just stared at the envelope, not speaking.

Letting out a sigh, James said, "Well are you going to open it, or do you want me to?"

Maria sat shifting her head ever so slightly from left to right, finally saying softly, "I'll open it."

Even then, it took several minutes before she reached out. But finally, she laid her fingers softly on one corner and turned it over. Running her finger under the glued flap, she opened the envelope. She closed her eyes as she took it out and sat that way as she unfolded the letter. Letting out a deep sigh, she opened her eyes. They went straight to the word, *congratulations*. Seeing that word her head dropped to the table.

"Oh my gosh, oh my gosh," she repeated over and over through tears.

James couldn't stand the suspense and grabbed the letter. He too saw the word, *congratulations*. He jumped from her chair, flew behind Maria and grabbed her by the waist. He began twirling her around the room, saying "You did it, baby! You did it!"

Indeed, she had. The next day she informed the executive director of Safe Harbor, Barbara Tomlinson, that she had been approved. She asked Barbara if there was an opening for a counselor and, if so, could she be considered. Three months later, Maria was working full-time as a licensed professional counselor at Safe Harbor.

About a year later, Maria got a call from Matt Cole, the board president of Safe Harbor. He asked if she would be willing to meet with him to discuss an idea he had. Of course, she agreed, and he asked if she was available in an hour. An hour later, he knocked on her office door. Matt explained that during the board meeting yesterday, Barbara had submitted her resignation. Her husband was being promoted at work, but his promotion meant they had to relocate to Dallas. Barbara knew they had to go through a formal process of seeking to hire a new director, but she said if they were smart, they would ask Maria to throw her hat in the arena. Matt was here asking her to do just that.

Maria was excited, nervous, and overwhelmed all at the same time. Of course, she would apply. She was excited that they even thought to ask her. She was overwhelmed at the idea of running a nonprofit. And she was nervous to get her hopes up too much in case she did not get the job. She told Matt she would definitely submit her resume and she did the next day. For the next two months the board interviewed a long line of hopeful new prospects. They narrowed the search down to two candidates, one of which was Maria. After the final interview, the board said she should hear something in the next day or two. Two days later, Matt knocked on her door and asked if she would be willing to accept the position as the new executive director. "Yes!" couldn't come out of her mouth fast enough.

The first few months in her new position Maria felt like that first semester in college—overwhelmed and eager to learn. She also knew she could do it. After all she had overcome, this was just another mountain to climb. She just needed to put on her mental mountain boots and set a course.

WHY THREE-POINT PARTNERSHIPS WORK

Partnerships work because each point in the partnership brings its unique perspectives, expertise, and resources. As said previously, nonprofits provide clients with proven effective programming. Businesses make a difference in communities with effective CSR efforts and have the added benefit of working with amazing women who are survivors or overcomers. And women are provided opportunities to new healthy futures, contributing to the community as well. The following are examples that show why three-point partnerships work.

Creating a Hiring Pipeline

The three-point partnership can work to create a hiring pipeline for businesses because the nonprofit organization provides women with the initial training in life and job skills. The nonprofit can also support the business's hiring efforts by screening the participants for the company. Such a partnership could replace the need for partnering with a hiring agency to fill some positions.

The business commits to pay women a fair wage for the work done. If the principles in this book are used in the business environment, the women would get opportunities for experiential learning and immediate leadership. The organization could support the women in translating their skills to business. At the same time, they will be creating additional value by adding diverse perspectives to the workforce.

Specifically, a social enterprise within a nonprofit organization can prepare women for jobs in a variety of industries, and businesses could rely on the organization to provide qualified and dependable employees. You see an example of this in chapter 5, when the business leaders come to the organization to try to learn what they are doing to create such a great pipeline of employees.

Train Managers

Together, the nonprofit organization and business can train managers to most effectively supervise women overcoming challenging pasts. Cheryl has provided trainings on many of the concepts in this book to businesses and not necessarily because they are hiring women with challenging pasts, but because the businesses saw value in these principles regardless of their employees' backgrounds.

Training mangers in the principles in this book will make them more effective with all employees but will also better prepare them to supervise women. Such preparation will help everyone, including the business, thrive. Again, the nonprofit organization in the partnership will often have more expertise about the needs of the population than the business. So, partnering on the training would produce the most effective results.

Create a Consortium

The interests of women like those in this book will vary widely in the work they find interesting. Likely, a one-to-one partnership between a business and a nonprofit organization will not provide enough diverse opportunities for the women. Therefore, nonprofit organizations supporting women like those profiled here should consider creating a consortium of corporate partners for the purpose of hiring. The consortium could include companies that would benefit from hiring these women and, ideally, require their supervisors to attend a manager training program as described in the previous section. Women are not required to work for companies in the consortium, but having a group of companies aligned on the principles needed for success would create a safe place for the women to consider starting their careers.

DO OVERS

Maria loved her job at Safe Harbor. She remembered the day she told James this job was what she was born to do. All her past experiences had prepared her for this job, and the women at the home were just like her in the past.

Safe Harbor was not a large nonprofit or even a large counseling program. They rented a building that was formerly a dentist's office and was converted to provide offices for five counselors. They were doing great work with clients, helping them overcome challenging issues, but they kept running into all the same barriers. Most of their clients were low income and many were trying to leave addictive and dangerous lifestyles. The barrier they ran into time and time again was the inability to earn enough money to escape that poverty and destruction. Maria was desperate to develop some type of wrap-around services that would provide their clients will skills to earn livable wages. But that would take money and more space than they had in their tiny offices.

Maria was sitting in her office, with a crack in the wall, when her assistant director knocked on her door to give her a postcard that came in the mail. It was from the Williams Foundation. It was announcing a grant opportunity for program development.

Maria was intrigued, so she looked up the website to see what it was all about. She only read half of the grant application when she realized, this was way too complicated. She didn't have the ability to write a grant that complicated. So, she closed the computer and started working on the budget for next year, still trying to think of a way to increase capacity.

The next day, Maria got an e-mail from a colleague. The e-mail was actually about the grant from Williams Foundation. Maria shot back a "Thanks, but no thanks" e-mail saying she didn't think she had the capacity to create a project like that. Two weeks later she was sitting at the local nonprofit leaders' luncheon and a colleague and good friend, Mark, told her he got a postcard about funding from the Williams Foundation, and she should consider applying. He handed her that same postcard about the grant.

"Yeah, I got that, too. And oddly, this is the third time I have heard about it." Maria said.

She went on to explain to Mark how difficult the application was. The application alone was fifteen pages. It required budgets, outputs, and pro forma statements. She didn't even know what a pro forma was. Mark knew all Maria had overcome, and he just looked at her and smiled.

"Don't be smiling at me that way. I can't do it!" Maria said trying not to smile back.

Mark said, "Come on Maria, when did you let something hard stop you?"

He was right. If that card crossed her path three times, maybe it was a sign. The next day she went back to the website and began the application. It took her a week to complete the grant. The grant was for $330,000 to purchase and renovate a new space. If approved, Safe Harbor would go from a five-office counseling service center to fifteen offices with a large room outfitted with computers, Wi-Fi, and everything needed to create a training center. Maria had no expectations they would get funded. She guessed on half the information she provided.

About three months later, she was driving across town running errands when her phone rang. She answered and the person on the other end was calling from the Williams Foundation. The voice on the phone told her congratulations that they had been approved for the grant. Maria instantly began crying and had to pull into a parking lot to calm herself down. After asking a few questions and hearing the details for the next steps, the call ended. Maria just sat in her car. She could not believe it had happened. Her dreams were coming true.

It took a lot of hard work to move from one location to the other and do all the work to get things operational, but it was so worth it. They had the ability to help so many men and women. And the clients in their counseling center were amazing. Maria decided the clients should be the main drivers of this new training program. She put out flyers announcing the new program asking for clients willing to build and shape this new project. Five clients signed up and Uplift was created. The first training developed was a collaborative between the clients and staff at Safe Harbor to train other organizations and churches on how to effectively work with people facing major obstacles such as poverty, addiction, or incarceration. And why not? Safe Harbor clients were experts on those subjects.

Uplift was a hit. They made money, and clients learned valuable skills, and the program was growing. Kathleen, one of the first to join Uplift, was a great cook and really wanted to start a small business where she made and delivered meals to busy families. She was telling Maria, if she only had access to a kitchen and a little money, she knew she could make a good living. That got Maria thinking. She picked up the phone and called Tom, the board chair to ask him what he thought about starting a program where they provided funding for women interested in starting their own business. He was instantly intrigued and said he loved the idea. After a few minutes, they decided they would ask the women at Uplift to put together some ideas of how they thought a program like this could work.

Two weeks later Kathleen handed Maria a folder. The cover said Freedom Capital Ventures. Inside were ideas the women had for launching small businesses. As Maria read, she was impressed. But like that day when she first saw the Williams Foundation postcard, she felt unqualified to help the women make this happen. She didn't know much about business, but even with the little she did know she saw major holes in the proposal. She told Kathleen as much.

"Well, we just need to find some businesspeople who can help us fill the holes." Kathleen said, adding, "We can do the digging, if they just tell us which holes to fill."

Maria busted out laughing. Kathleen was right. Maria had connections to business leaders. She decided to go to the next Business Leader luncheon that was held monthly at the local country club. She sat next to Jonathan Marshall, the owner of a large supply company. She was about to tell him her idea about Freedom Capital Ventures when the group chair asked if anyone had any news they wanted to share. Maria decided to tell the group the idea the women at Uplift created.

> *"We can do the digging, if they just tell us which holes to fill."*

As soon as she finished laying out the plans Jonathan leaned over and said, "I want to give $10,000 for the microloans."

Maria's eyes nearly popped out of their sockets. She finally said, "Jonathan, we don't even have a full program yet. We are not ready for that kind of money."

"Well then, I want to help develop the program." He shot back.

Three weeks later, Maria, Kathleen, two other women from Uplift, Jonathan, and two other influential business leaders were sitting around a table in Jonathan's boardroom hashing out details for Freedom Capital Ventures. Three more meetings over the next few months and Freedom Capital Ventures was a reality. They now had the means and process to allow women to apply for small loans to launch their own business.

Kathleen was the first to apply. The business leaders that partnered with the women now acted as the "shark tank" called the Leadership Resource Team (LRT) to review their business proposals. Kathleen's business plan was good, but the team had some concerns about a few areas and suggested she look into and come back with a stronger proposal. She did just that and a month later they were reviewing her revised plan. Ron Crawford, the LRT member who owned a successful restaurant smiled and said he was impressed. He went on to say, she had better revisions than he had thought of.

"You are going to make a run for my money" he laughed.

But the team agreed. The plan was solid, Kathleen's business would be solid, and it was unanimous; they all approved her $3,200 loan to launch Kathleen's Country Kitchen. Kathleen actually let out a squeal when she heard the news. A squeal that was quickly followed by tears. Maria reached over and put her arms around her as she cried tears of joy.

Maria was so proud of the participants at Uplift. They saw something that would be good, and they went after it. She helped where she could, but the most important thing that she brought to the table was her connection to business leaders who would help them. She was talking about that with Jonathan after the next LRT meeting, reviewing the second business plan from a woman at Uplift. He said it was exciting, but she needed to give herself credit. She was the one that saw something that didn't exist when she created Uplift. He told her she was a pioneer, and he was grateful to be on the journey with her. Maria never thought of herself as a pioneer but maybe she was. She also realized she didn't need to do anymore pioneering. She would turn that responsibility over to the men and women at Uplift.

Two months later, Kathleen was ready for her soft launch of Kathleen's Country Kitchen. All her meals would be ordered through the website she created and would be delivered. She worked hard creating healthy but delicious food. The hardest part was finding a commercial kitchen she could use. There was a small restaurant that closed several years back. In fact, every restaurant that tried to open in that location failed. But Kathleen didn't need a restaurant, she only needed a kitchen, and she convinced the owner to lease her the kitchen. And the day it opened, the Chamber of Commerce was there with a red ribbon. Kathleen asked Maria to stand with her as she did the ribbon cutting. Both women were weeping as the ribbon floated to the ground.

With tears in her eyes Maria turned to Kathleen and said, "This is your future. And you know what, there's the door."

7

CHALLENGES AND SOLUTIONS

Certainly, we present success stories in this book. But we don't want to leave any illusions that this is easy work—for the women recovering from previously marginalized identities (incarceration, addiction, poverty, sexual exploitation, or abuse) or the business leaders offering support. However, the problems many organizations and individuals doing this work encounter can be addressed and overcome. To do so may require some challenging new mindsets, but it can be done if you are ready to try.

In this chapter, we address the most common challenges facing organizations hoping to help and facing the women working to overcome a challenging past. Frankly, these are the issues we often see organizations use as an excuse for not helping or a barrier that stops their help from being most effective.

CHALLENGE 1: WOMEN'S CRIMINAL RECORDS

When Shannon started her research exploring women's experiences exiting the sex trade, she was convinced criminal records would be a significant barrier for women in trying to find legally recognized work.

It's a challenge but not an insurmountable one. Criminal records pose two challenges—one actual and the other perceived.[1] Some women did face barriers to their desired employment as a result of their criminal records. However, far more often, women's fears, or perceptions, that their criminal records would prevent them from getting a job was more of a barrier. This is not to say, there are no challenges to employment for individuals with felony convictions. There will be some employers that because of their industry cannot hire felons. But many others can. Even in areas where there are restrictions, sometimes those restrictions are negotiable like we saw in Maria's story.

We have seen nonprofit organizations assume women can't get jobs or housing because of having felonies. When service providers provide misinformation to clients, the assumption can stifle their progress and limit the support such women could receive. Presenting erroneous information harms their ability to move forward. If a trusted advisor confirms someone's fear about her criminal record interfering with her ability to secure employment, then the formerly incarcerated woman would be even less likely to apply for a position she might otherwise get. When this happens, we are actually harming those we are hoping to help.

You saw a story similar to this in chapter 5, when Diana attended a conference and the speaker said someone with a felony conviction couldn't qualify for government housing or receive financial aid for school. Cheryl has had that same experience. Even when she tried to correct the information, the group was resistant to listening. Further, the housing program Cheryl ran for eighteen years also applied for HUD funding that was granted to provide housing for formerly incarcerated women while they were completing college education that they were able to attend through financial aid.

Solutions

1. Companies: Companies could consider hiring women with criminal records. The practice may require some policy changes, but it is possible. In chapter 8, we share recent commitments large corporations have made to postpone asking about criminal records in the hiring process. There are many amazing women

that employers will miss out on due to restrictive policies regarding criminal records.

2. Organizations: Organizations supporting women should work with companies willing to hire employees with criminal records. Most importantly, don't be that organization at the conference that Cheryl attended. Don't discourage women from pursuing employment based on their record. Try to find a solution to move forward. Organizations can help women clear their criminal records, or they can help them find companies that will hire them despite their record.

3. Women:
   a. Clearing a criminal record can be difficult but not impossible. Shannon interviewed one participant who had an arrest record. She was arrested but never charged. She dreamed of being a teacher. When she was about halfway through her teaching degree, she applied to be a substitute teacher. Her dreams were dashed when the school district ran a background check and would not employ her because of the arrest. She changed her degree to psychology, graduated, and attended graduate school to become a counselor. But during graduate school, a local attorney heard of her situation and offered to help. After a few months, the arrest was removed from her record. Once the record was cleared, she took the necessary courses to supplement her degree to become a teacher. She is now a middle school teacher.
   b. Apply for jobs, even ones you don't think you will get. We have seen too many women miss, or almost miss, opportunities that were actually available to them because they were afraid their record might impede their employment.

CHALLENGE 2: SELF-DISCLOSURE

In Shannon's research, she found women were more likely to self-disclose when first exiting the sex trade. One of the participants said, often when someone is first in recovery they are focused on their "uniqueness." It's a strange combination of pride and shame or at least shame disguised as pride that made it hard for women to resist sharing their pasts.

Another participant in the study shared a story showing her evolution from frequent self-disclosure to never self-disclosing as the years went by after exiting. Her willingness to self-disclose earlier after exiting impacted the way she was treated at work. She said,

> I was really honest early on, TOO honest. And [woman working at the organization] would be like, "Watch what you're saying now, because one day you are going to have a life and you're not going to want that everywhere around." And I'm like, "Nah, I'm good, girl, I'm good." . . . And I get that today. I'm like, "Yeah, I don't want everyone to know that." But I didn't get that then. . . . My other boss . . . I self-disclosed to her for 3 hours. . . . She hired me . . . but then later on, it also kind of went against me sometimes, because she knew too much . . . I don't self-disclose like that [now] . . . like nobody at my gym, nobody at my work. They don't know anything. They just know me as, she's getting her master's degree, she's married, basic stuff. And I have just had to learn when was it appropriate, not appropriate.

The participant also talked about being in a college class for counseling, and the professor was talking about trauma. She raised her hand and told her entire class about being raped by two men at gunpoint and knife point. She said she didn't think anything was wrong with sharing that, until the whole class looked at her like she was crazy.

Employers looking to support women in transitioning from the sex trade or other identities society has historically marginalized will have to navigate self-disclosure with care.

Solutions

Supporting survivors in navigating self-disclosure will be even more critical when they have newly exited. The following are some strategies for doing so.

1. Companies: Train managers to maintain survivors' confidentiality. Have firm policies against gossip. Care around self-disclosure is particularly important when companies have partnered

with organizations to hire women with particular identities. For example, if a company partners with an organization for battered women, the company would need to ensure survivors' past remains confidential.

2. Organizations: Advise women not to self-disclose. Someday the world may be more accepting, but now self-disclosure can be a liability. Also, advise women to leave a company if they have self-disclosed, and it becomes a barrier holding them back.

3. Women: Exercise care in self-disclosure. As the participant quoted in this section found out, even a trusted employer subconsciously placed limitations on the survivor based on her previous identity. However, recognize that avoiding self-disclosure becomes easier over time. If you disclosed early on, know you are not alone. You may have to leave an organization if your previous self-disclosure is impacting your future opportunities there. The participant had to leave the organization, which was okay. It led to much richer employment opportunities for her.

CHALLENGE 3: DEMONSTRATING INAPPROPRIATE WORK BEHAVIOR

Often, as Shannon found in her study with women exiting the sex trade, women recovering from challenging pasts had to relearn how to talk, dress, and act appropriately at work. In their efforts to relearn behaviors, some participants learned the hard way by being fired from their first jobs after exiting.

Related to talk, one participant who was fired from her first job for cussing out customers said,

> After being in that mess for twenty years, I didn't even know how to speak English properly. It's just slang. Most people didn't even understand what I was saying. . . . And I'm so awful about it. I have a potty mouth. You hear me. I am working on learning how to be a lady. I want to be that person. I'm not there yet obviously, but it is what it is.

Learning how to talk for mainstream society was critical in their recovery and took some time.

Like in Cara's story, many of the participants had to learn how to dress. They often learned from watching others, like organizational leaders. For example, one participant said,

> Well, watching women like [the women working at the organization] and the way they dress and understanding that they were not showing their boobs to everyone and they did not have a whale tail [G-string] up the back. And I was like, "Hold on. Hmmm. Classy, not classy; classy, not classy." Starting to look at what was appropriate. So, I think it was just by really being observant as to the women I wanted to more mirror. . . . Also, when we were teaching that computer class, I got to see. One of the girls showed up with a John one day and she was trying to pull her clothes on as she was coming into the computer class. And I was like, "Hmmm. Do I want to be that girl or do I want to look like [women working at the organization]." . . . She was late coming to computer class. When I opened the door, she was out there with a John in the truck and I was like, "Don't miss that. Don't miss that at all. I don't miss that."

Organization leaders were influential, but so were other participants a little ahead in their recovery. Another participant talked about the influence other women in the house that supported her exit had on the way she dressed. She said,

> Even the other women in the house would really influence each other, because I remember. . . . I just dressed like a hoochy everywhere I went. And I remember walking out, which is so far removed from me today, I can't even believe it. I remember walking out of the house and this girl was like, "You're going to wear that to church?" And I was like, "Yeah." And she was like, "Really? Your boobs are hanging out. You really think everybody needs to see that?" . . . It's like I didn't even know. Like I didn't. And I was like, "Wow, my boobs shouldn't be hanging out?" I didn't even know. Just completely unaware. Oh, I need to cover them. I need to cover my boobs in public. Wow, what a concept.

Challenges related to appearance were not limited to dress.

Another participant had many tattoos, including visible tattoos on her face and hands. She was aware of the challenge her tattoos presented in gaining employment. She said about some employers:

Some were like, "I can't hire you with the felonies." But really it was the tattoos, trust me. My hands, you can't cover that stuff up with makeup. So, I was like, "Geez this sucks." So, I was turned down by everyone. And I think there were a few that I could have gotten a job even with eight felonies, but not looking like it.[2]

The participant had undergone tattoo removal over the years, so her appearance was more consistent with professional expectations.

Other work behavior that women had to learn over time was to be consistent and reliable by being on time and not missing work. One participant described how her boss helped teach her responsibility to work through consequences:

He would have to really school me on all of that stuff. I did not know. If I was late, "Guess what? You don't work today." After a couple times, I need that money. I'll be here on time. You know he never fired me but when I cussed him out. . . . "Do not come back to work until next week and you need to think about what happened." I was like a little kid.

Solutions

1. Companies: As demonstrated in chapter 6, partner with organizations that provide women with effective job training. Set clear expectations and establish effective accountability for all employees.
2. Organizations: Provide classes on professional dress and behavior but also provide practice. Implementing a social enterprise in your organization provides women with tangible practice inside the safety of the organization that will prepare them for future jobs.
3. Women: Get advice from others. Similar to Maria's story, one of the participants in Shannon's study sought advice on what to wear to her hearing for becoming a licensed professional counselor. She did not like the outfit recommended to her, but the advice helped her tremendously because she looked professional when she went before the panel. Emphasizing the importance of dress seems superficial, but it does matter in a professional setting. The way women dressed in the sex trade to promote their sex appeal did not translate to acceptance at work or an increase

in self-worth in a mainstream environment. Self-worth came not from looking sexy but from work-related accomplishments. As one participant said, she realized she "was capable of so much more. Not needing to be validated, like, 'Oh you're pretty,' but 'Oh you're intellectual, oh, you can think.' You know what I mean, and those things were really important for me."[3]

CHALLENGE 4: TOLERATING INAPPROPRIATE BEHAVIOR FROM OTHERS AT WORK

Frequently, women did not know what to expect from employers. In the previous section, we talked about how they did not always demonstrate behavior appropriate for work. This section explores the fact that women overcoming a challenging past also often do not know the standard for appropriate behavior from their coworkers. For example, some participants experienced sexual harassment at work, tolerated dirty jokes, or were cussed out by their bosses and didn't know such experiences were unacceptable.

One participant experienced sexual harassment at work. She said:

> And the guy, the owner, started acting weird and he had asked me to go on a trip or do something and I went back to group and I ended up telling [my counselor] . . . and she was like that's sexual harassment. My comment was, "How is that any different from the rest of my life?" I could not even recognize sexual harassment. . . . Sometimes in the early stages of exiting, we don't recognize workplace abuses and things that are illegal, because it's so similar to things we've always been dealing with.

The participant did not recognize the behavior as problematic without support from someone else.

Two participants described being yelled at or "cussed out" by their bosses, which they did not think was abnormal or unacceptable. Cara's story about the strip club comment was inspired by a common interaction one of the participants described about her work in a male-dominated industry. Unlike with Cara, the participant did not feel she had the power to say anything. When sex jokes came up in the office, the woman often would laugh along uncomfortably. She said, "And I'm like oh my God, you really said that. I'm not sure how hard I should laugh."

Solutions

1. Company: Do not tolerate a culture that perpetuates outdated jokes or conversations demeaning to any population—in this case, women. The #MeToo movement has placed pressure on organizations to implement such policies. In the appendix, we offer an assessment to help your company determine if you are ready to hire women like those in this book, who can positively impact your organization. A large part of that readiness is checking your company's culture. What you tolerate from employees influences your culture as much as what you encourage.

2. Organization: Most coaching we see provided by organizations is focused on the women's behavior. Be sure to include coaching on what the women you support should expect from employers. It is important employers don't perpetuate marginalization or the oppression a woman experienced from a previous perpetrator. Natural power imbalances occur in the workplace between supervisor and employee, arming women with appropriate expectations will help protect them.

3. Women: Often women we meet are not even aware they are being harassed or discriminated against because it was so inherent in their former lives. Having a mentor can help you determine issues that need to be reported to supervisors, or human resources, depending on the reporting structure within the company. It can be scary to bring concerns to light. You may feel like you are risking your job, but most often it would be better to leave an organization with a culture that perpetuates marginalization than to stay and hope things change.

CHALLENGE 5: RELAPSE

We use the term *relapse* in the traditional sense of the word—related to returning to drug or alcohol addiction after a period of recovery.

Relapse to addictions was a challenge for many of the women in the sex trade and for those who experienced incarceration and poverty. We also use the term to describe women's reentry back into the sex trade after an exit. Factors contributing to their relapse were unique, which are discussed after a broader look at the challenge of drug addiction.

Drug Addiction

Of course, employees relapsing is a risk for those employing anyone who has recovered from drug or alcohol addiction. However, companies can work to provide support that can minimize the likelihood.

Many of the women we met had long-term issues with substance use. Although it is always desirable that anyone in recovery maintains sobriety on the first attempt, it is rare. However, it is important to state that when the principles in this book are used, in Cheryl's experience, relapse episodes decreased significantly. And when relapse did happen, most women were able to self-adjust back to sobriety with no external intervention or support.

Specific to women exiting the sex trade, drug addiction was rarely mentioned by the participants in Shannon's study as a reason for reentry into the sex trade. But it is also important to recognize that substance use is common for those engaged in the sex trade. To understand the full scope of relapse for women exiting the sex trade, and not just relapse into drug use, it is important to know the two most common factors to which women most often attributed their return into the sex trade: money and the lifestyle mindset.

The Money.   Most of the women interviewed said money, and anxiety around money, drew them back into the sex trade. As one participant said, the money "was far more of a relapse for me than the dope ever could be." The money was a draw back into the sex trade, in part, because women knew they could make more money in the sex trade than they could in the employment available to them after exiting. As one participant said,

> I still live with [the thought that] I could go to the corner and make $1,000 and everything is going to be fine. . . . How do you think it felt

for me going from making $1,000 a day down to $8 an hour? $8 an hour? I was like, "My f°#ing check for the whole week was what I made in an hour."

She had been out of the sex trade the longest and was the most vocal about the inequities of the sex trade, including pay. For another participant, the pull was more related to anxiety about not having enough money. She said:

> I gave up other things, but there was that one thing. I don't know why. I mean, I guess because it was my security blanket. Cause, if I want money and I don't have it, I know how to get it. It's just a walk away. I just need to take a little walk and I'll come back with it. . . . I told my husband too. . . . "I have to have money. You don't understand. I have to have money. So when my dollars start to go down. You need to be man enough to say, 'Honey, do you need anything?' And throw me dollars, because my mind will go left." Shoot, my husband don't want to share his money? I'm gonna get my money somewhere else. . . . I'm afraid of what I, I don't want to cheat on him and I don't think I ever would. I don't think I would. I'm afraid that I would be in that situation. What if I don't have no money? Would I be tempted to look to the left or to the right? That's a scary thought, because I don't want to cheat on that man. . . . I just don't want to look like I'm broke, cause that kind of feeling makes me itchy. It's crazy, I don't understand it.

About half of the participants disclosed continuing to engage in the sex trade after they transitioned to a housing program. Disengaging from how they knew how to interact with men and how they knew how to make money was extremely difficult.

For many of them, their first jobs after exiting did not pay a living wage. Those jobs also were undesirable. We shared a few examples of such jobs in chapter 6 that described how participants hated their first jobs. They were not making enough money and they "had numbers memorized," meaning they could call a John to make more money faster. The adjustment was challenging. In addition to the draw to the money, in part because of low pay and because of a lack of desirable work options, women were also pulled back into the sex trade by what one participant coined the "mindset of the lifestyle."

The Lifestyle Mindset.   Before we talk about the lifestyle mind-set, it's important to investigate the word *lifestyle* briefly. Years before Shannon started her study, she started researching the sex trade. In her research, she found a plethora of scholarly articles debating the words *sex work* and *prostitution*. As in, should the act of exchanging sex for money (or other goods and services of value) be called *sex work* or *prostitution*. On one side of the argument, *sex work* is considered a viable form of income that some women can pursue with agency. On the other side is *prostitution*, which scholars consider a human rights' violation. In an effort to be inclusive of all perspectives, Shannon planned to start each interview with the question, "Do you use the term *sex work* or *prostitution* to describe selling sex for money?"

The first interview Shannon did was a pilot interview with a woman who exited the sex trade. She had volunteered to test out the questions and provide feedback. When Shannon asked the first question the woman broke out in laughter. Then said, "Neither." This is not the type of work academics can do from an ivory tower or else they spend too much time debating the terms *sex work* and *prostitution* (some of this debate is warranted and healthy), while those with the most expertise—the women who engaged in the sex trade—don't identify with either term. She said, most often people refer to it as the *lifestyle* (followed by *turning tricks* and *hustling*).

The lifestyle. That's a powerful term with serious significance. *The lifestyle* implies an all-encompassing way of living. That's what it's like to be in the sex trade, an all-encompassing lifestyle. You hear it when they talk about the way it changed their speech and dress but, most importantly, in the way it changed their mindset.

In the middle of conducting the study, Shannon attended a conference on sex trafficking. A detective was talking about a young woman who was testifying against her pimp. The prosecutor had coached the witness in answering questions and thought she was well-prepared to bring a convincing prosecution against her trafficker. During the defense's questioning, they asked the young woman about a time she stole a car, no doubt to discredit her witness against the pimp. It worked. Her entire testimony had been unemotional and lacked energy. Then she lit up when she started talking about stealing the car. She smiled and told the story to the jury with all of its drama, with some added for affect no doubt. The prosecution and detectives were so disappointed in her. Shannon just thought, "and there it is, *the lifestyle mindset.*"

The lifestyle mindset is many things, one of which is the rush of it all—even of the chaos. One participant called the excitement that comes with the lifestyle mindset the "bling-bling."[4] For some, the bling-bling came from the thrill, even the thrill of dangerous situations. For example, as one participant described, "being caught by the police or getting beat up by a sex buyer, whatever it is." The excitement of the lifestyle is a stark contrast to all that follows. As the participant said, "When you are out in sex trade, there's constantly bright lights, whoop, whoop, danger, scare, fight, flight. You got all of these things going on and I remember getting into recovery and thinking well f*@k, this is boring."[5]

The women had to learn everything again, but they also had to completely change their lifestyle. As one participant said, it all had to change—"people, place, and things."[6] The transition was dramatic and meant being bored in the mundane of their new lifestyle.

Solutions

1. Companies: Related to preventing relapse into the sex trade, pay a fair wage and offer dignified jobs. Looking back to translation factor, remember that women overcoming challenging pasts have extensive and unique skills they bring to companies—like resilience, the ability to motivate others, and a strong work ethic. Companies can also support women seeking to maintain sober lifestyles by offering flexible schedules that allow them to attend AA or NA meetings. Policies providing a second chance to those who are battling recovery can also have a positive impact. For example, a second chance policy could allow an employee to take a leave of absence to attend rehab after relapse. Such policies are most successful when they include specific expectations and conditions for returning to work.

2. Organizations: To address relapse into the sex trade, as an organization you can teach the women you support sustainable job skills. Unfortunately, most organizations supporting women teach them to make something like jewelry, household goods,

candles, or soaps. These are not economically sustainable skills. It is difficult to make a living wage with these skills. One of the participants knew it. She said, "The organization supporting her exit lets you make [candles], and I was like I can't make [candles] for a living." She didn't know what she was going to do when she left the organization, but she was not allowed to work while she was there and the only skill she developed was making candles. The lack of sustainability in that job skill made her nervous. There are organizations in the world, like Prajwala in India that teach women more traditionally masculine job skills—like carpentry, plumbing, and electrical skills. They are extremely successful because these skills are more economically sustainable. Whatever skills they learn have to be able to support them financially because the anxiety about money is too much for most. For women overcoming addiction, organizations can provide opportunities for women to connect with recovery programs like NA, AA, and Celebrate Recovery. Some organizations require women to participate in a recovery program, while receiving services or housing. Such practices allow women to build support systems to take into their lives and the workplace.

3. Women: Learn the skills needed to do a job that will sustain you financially. Consider going back to school, if needed to gain additional skills. We have seen so many women go from prison to college with great success. If you have not already, you can, too. Related specifically to drug addiction, ensure you are constantly getting the support you need through counseling, AA or NA, and so forth.

CHALLENGE 6: CHALLENGES MANAGING MENTAL HEALTH AND EMOTIONS

Managing mental health is important for all of us. Specifically, we are learning more about the impact of mental health on work performance. For example, one study projected "monthly depression-related worker productivity losses had human capital costs of nearly $2 billion" in the United States.[7]

Women who have overcome addition, incarceration, engagement in the sex trade, or poverty may have some unique mental health challenges. Many of the women included in Shannon's study struggled with symptoms of post-traumatic stress disorder (PTSD), depression, and anxiety. The most common challenge, though, was simply a lack of self-worth.

Self-Worth

In talking about feeling a lack of self-worth, one participant said,

> I was just broken. Even though I was out of it, I was an empty shell and so that was probably the hardest part. I still didn't believe I was worthy of change . . . and even still, still I struggle with self-esteem. I'm trying to unpack my brain and take control. But when you're powerless or feel powerless for so long, it's hard to empower yourself. I still question that and I'm out 5 years.

When I was with the participant, she showed me a piece she drew in art therapy—beautiful and poignant—a sketch of a woman with her lips sown together. She said, "That's like how I felt. Like I had no voice." Another participant said,

> I didn't know what I was good *at* anymore. I didn't know what I was good *for* anymore.[8] . . . Because you get a lot of that taken from you, beaten out of you, when you're in the life. I don't know, I don't know how to dream. I don't know how, because I didn't think I would make it this far. I stopped dreaming. I stopped having goals, because you don't set your goals. Somebody sets them for you. You achieve somebody else's bar, you don't set your own bar, you don't achieve your own bar.

For so long, many of the women had found their self-worth in the sex trade.

We shared the following quote in chapter 4, but it warrants repeating in this context. A third participant talked about finding her esteem in men picking her on the street. She said,

> It was also a way I felt validated that I was pretty. Like I always felt attractive when they chose me or something like that. It was really sick . . . my self-esteem, my self-worth were really wrapped around men

finding me attractive in a certain way. . . . Standing on the street corner out there and when the guys drove by and picked you, I was like, "I'm pretty. Gotta go." And no. I mean, I got into so many situations that were horrific thinking they picked me, oh they picked me. And it validated that I was somehow okay or good enough.

After exiting, work impacted the women's self-worth significantly.

Making money on their own and working built women's self-worth. When asked what helped build her self-worth the most, one participant answered, "That I can make honest dollars. I can make honest dollars . . . on my own, not from other people holding my money. But on my own."[9] Similarly, as we stated in chapter 4, another participant talked about work giving her a new purpose. She said,

> You start to build self-worth and self-esteem, because you have a job and you're doing something. . . . Having a purpose, feeling needed, feeling like I was doing something productive, like I was a productive member of society . . . and not feeling like I was on the opposite side. Starting to feel like I was on the right side, I think really helped . . . integrate me into society.[10]

She gained the experiences that made her feel "on the right side" and integrated back into society by working at the social enterprise supported by the organization helping her exit. She has been able to translate not only the skills she learned there but also the esteem she gained into a successful career.

PTSD, Depression, and Anxiety

We take care in presenting these challenges because we are not mental health experts. However, many of the women disclosed experiencing symptoms of PTSD, depression, and anxiety. It is important also to note that these challenges did not stop any of the women. We see some organization treat the women as if they are fragile. We have never met a more resilient, strong population—*ever*. Kid gloves are not necessary, but awareness of the principles in this book can help support women in their journey, such as restorative justice and trauma-informed care.

Remember the example in Emmie's story. It was the expectation of outsiders that women in recovery or in the process of transformation are somehow fragile. Of course, as seen in the stories of all the women, they are not fragile at all. In Cheryl's experience, a better word would be *vulnerable*. At times, they feel vulnerable, which can feel uncomfortable. Vulnerable in that someone might use them, or judge them, or see a part of their former life that brushes up against shame. In fact, their ability to push through the vulnerability is a clear indicator they are indeed strong.

As mentioned, many of the women struggled with self-worth. They may connect their current failures, small or large, with their self-worth and make them feel like others see them as less than. Saying they are fragile and giving failure such magnitude leaves them vulnerable. Pushing past that vulnerability takes courage and persistence to fight the lies in their head saying, "You can't do this. You will always be a failure." Silencing those lies and moving forward takes incredible strength. It may or may not make a difference, but the comment about fragility was made by a man. I would question if this same male colleague would say the same for men in recovery or reentry into society after incarceration.

Related to PTSD, some women experience nightmares, a tendency toward catastrophic thinking, paranoia, fear, refusal of treatment, and lack of trust. Some of the women also disclose struggling with depression, but again, their resilience helps them manage the related challenges. One overcomer said:

> I give myself like periods of time where I'm allowed to be depressed, because I think that comes along with recovery. You're going to be depressed. But I give myself like, this is how many days I'm going to allow myself to lay on the couch and then I'm going to get active and attempt to come out of my funk.

Solutions

1. Companies: Related to self-worth, employers adopting the translation factor had the greatest impact on women's self-worth. As you saw with Maggie's story, having an employer who

respected her previous experiences and helped her translate was powerful. The women also found it helpful when they had employer-provided counseling benefits, including paid time off to participate in counseling.

2. Organizations: We recommend organizations supporting women adopt trauma-informed care practices. However, we do not recommend coddling women. We have seen quite a few organizations who do not let women work while they are in recovery. Some don't let them leave the recovery home, except to go to church. With the positive impact work and making money has on women's self-worth, growth and development, and self-efficacy in their ability to provide for themselves, we do not find this protection to be necessary. In fact, it can have the opposite effect intended.

3. Women: Get out there and start working, make mistakes, and learn from them. Find people who will encourage you. Translate the skills you learned on the streets—the resilience you gained and the work ethic you developed—into your current work. You have something others don't, which makes you incredible and unique.

CHALLENGE 7: INCLUSION

Challenges we face today with inclusion impact us all. Certainly, companies struggle to create more inclusive environments, and many nonprofits must work to overcome biases—their own, their donors', and their clients'. Women who inspired the stories in this book were impacted by issues of inclusion as well. Most of them experienced some aspect of their social identities that were historically marginalized in our culture. For some, aspects of their social identities intersected to magnify the marginalization—such as race, class, sexual orientation, gender identity, religious beliefs, disability, and so on. Both authors of this book have never experienced issues related to race, sexual orientation, or gender identity because both are White, heterosexual, cisgender females. But both know and worked with

women who were directly affected by issues such as racism and homophobia.

In the nonprofit organization Cheryl ran, issues of homophobia
and racism—conscious or unconscious—arose. First, related to homophobia, the housing program Cheryl ran assisted women from
the LBGTQ+ community, which created some tension with the faith
community. Leaders from the faith community expressed concerns
about the housing program assisting women from the LGBTQ+ community. There was no way the nonprofit was going to discriminate
against women based on their sexual orientation or not serve them on
that basis. However, laypeople and leaders from the faith community,
who often also served as donors and volunteers, did not always share
the same value and withdrew funding.

Another example is related to racism: each year, the organization
hosted an event to raise funds locally. And each year, they produced
a video sharing the stories of the women. The nonprofit was intentional in sharing stories that represented all the women they served.
One year they interviewed four women for the event. One member
of the board that was working to edit the videos wanted a certain
woman's story removed. The one he wanted removed was the only
Black woman interviewed. When Cheryl pointed that out, the board
member explained that the suggestion about removal had nothing to
do with the color of the woman, but her story didn't seem as real as
the others. In reality, her story did not seem as real to him, as a White
male. Her story was not removed.

These biases, whether overt or unconscious, impact the ability of
women to overcome the challenges facing them.

Solutions

1. Companies: Of course, companies should work toward diverse,
   equitable, and inclusive work environments and hiring practices.
   Specific to this book, adopting restorative justice practices can
   create environments more inclusive of all voices, even those
   who typically are not heard. Further, companies can vet their
   nonprofit partnerships based on how inclusive the organization

is in offering services. Work to partner with organizations with diverse clients who do not turn clients away based on their social identities. Further, business leaders should work to monitor their use of power. It is easy to dismiss the more marginalized perspectives as a leader who believes they have all the answers. Those with power must be willing to listen and to share decision-making and leadership responsibility so diverse perspectives and voices are represented.

2. Organizations: Create policies that do not discriminate against women for their social identities. For nonprofit leaders who have experienced privilege, especially White privilege, do the work to better understand the issues facing the diverse women served. Use the principles of this book and give those served a direct voice to address issues they face both in the community and within the organization. Make sure staff and board leadership reflects the same diversity of the clients. And like in business, it is important to give equal voice and leadership to all involved.

3. Women: Seek organizations and companies that are inclusive of you. You deserve support, and there are organizations out there who will accept you. You are worthy of finding them. As we have said in other sections of this book, what you have to offer is significant. You may have some of the same skill sets as your colleagues, but in addition to those, you bring diverse experiences based on your background and culture. You bring your unique heritage and insight that is much needed in business today. Finally, women we have talked to with diverse identities recommend having people in your life who will encourage you and help you when you face challenging issues. This could include finding a mentor who understands the issues you face and who will provide support through challenges. For instance, if you are a Latina woman find a Latina mentor who has achieved goals similar to those you want to achieve; relationships that can facilitate mutual encouragement and support.

In addition to challenges women face, each of the principles have aspects that can cause difficulty in implementation. We cover those challenges and associated solutions in the following section.

CHALLENGES IMPLEMENTING THE PRINCIPLES

This section will address the challenges of implementing the principles outlined in chapters 1 through 6: experiential learning, immediate leadership opportunities, entrepreneurial culture, translation factor, restorative justice, and partnerships. Some of these challenges were referenced in those chapters but are worth restating.

There are two challenges that apply in implementing all of the principles. First, all of the principles require time to implement, which can be challenging for all stakeholders. Some of the principles require an initial investment of time to implement. For other principles, like experiential learning, the approach itself will take more time in the short term than alternative strategies. As we stated in chapter 1, trying to figure something out independently will take longer than the traditional approach of providing an employee with directions. However, allowing employees time to learn on their own or search out possible answers is a must. The employees will retain the answer more effectively than if the supervisor always provides the answer. The initial time investment is worth the ultimate payoff of the employee improving more rapidly over time.

Second, all of the principles may require a shift in culture and existing mental models. Some organizations and individuals may be more ready to embrace the principles than others. Some principles may be easier to adopt and others harder. The challenges might be opposite for someone else. We have created an assessment in the appendix, which organizations can use to determine how ready they are to hire women overcoming challenging pasts. Organizations committed to adopting the principles will need to remain diligent in implementing the principles and holding teams accountable for their execution. There are also challenges specific to individual principles that are outlined in this next section, along with solutions to address each challenge.

Challenges in Experiential Learning

Quality control presents challenges with experiential learning. When learning a new concept, skill, or process, there will always be a learning curve. The level of proficiency at the beginning will be lower than over time. Although it is understandable that an employee may not master a skill immediately, mastery must be the goal. Balancing the time needed to increase capacity and proficiency with the clearly articulated expectation of high quality and mastery can be challenging.

Another challenge in implementing experiential learning is resisting the temptation to take over when an employee is struggling. Of course, some guidance can be useful, but we must resist our natural reaction to intervene with too many instructions or assistance. The outcome is well worth practicing patience when productivity and proficiency increase.

Solution

1. Companies: To combat quality control issues in an experiential learning environment, companies can benchmark with periodic check-ins. Such practices will ensure progress is being made. Further, check-ins allow less experienced employees to learn from more seasoned employees. The second challenge is more difficult. It takes mental awareness and commitment to the concept to allow employees to both struggle and learn. When someone is struggling to learn new content, remind yourself to allow them time to find solutions independently.

2. Organizations: Evaluate existing programming to ensure clients are not just learning but also gaining experiences. Many organizations follow a traditional volunteer/staff-led format. Implementing practices like Food for Futures in chapter 6 can move learning from lecture to experiential, where clients practice the material they are learning.

3. Women: Start learning new things on your own. If you don't have access to a computer or the Internet, check out the public library. Create a roadmap to accomplish a dream and learn what you need to make it happen. Resources like Google and YouTube are wonderful tools to learn new things. The best resource is practice—gain experiences and learn from any mistakes. Find people who will encourage your learning but not give you all the answers.

Challenges in Immediate Leadership Opportunities

Power can get in the way when implementing immediate leadership opportunities. Giving control over to someone else can feel challenging. Doing so requires trust. On the flip side, when some individuals are given power for the first time, it can become intoxicating and lead to either intentional or unintentional power abuse.

Solution

1. Companies: The best solution is to start small to build trust. Start by giving someone a small task or small stakes project to lead. The opportunity will be a great learning experience for the employee and supervisor. Incrementally add more leadership opportunities as trust is built and both parties are comfortable. If an emerging leader assumes too much power, a simple role-play can help, such as asking questions like:

   • Think of a time someone with authority used their power in a way that was unhealthy or unproductive.
     ◦ How did you feel when that happened?
     ◦ Can you see yourself falling into a similar situation?

   It is also helpful to set clear expectations of what power the employee has in the area of leadership and also in relation to other employees. The simple fact of addressing power at the beginning of leadership opportunities can create an awareness for the participant.
2. Organizations: Evaluate existing programming to determine areas where clients can lead and lead early after entering your program. If there are no places to allow clients to lead in existing programming, create a space where clients can lead. For example, survivors could lead small groups for the purpose of reflection, a task force to develop new services, or as peer-to-peer coaches. Clients can develop and teach new curriculum based on the needs they identified in the population.
3. Women: Look for opportunities to lead. If you don't currently have the opportunity to lead in your job or the organization where you are receiving services, look for other places. You can

volunteer to lead in civic groups in your community, nonprofit organizations, in NA or AA if you are a member, or at churches to name a few opportunities. If you have never seen yourself as a leader, ask yourself why? Everyone is good at something. When you realize your gift, look for ways to lead using that gift.

Challenges in Entrepreneurial Culture

Old mindsets create the greatest barriers to an entrepreneurial culture. Many businesses tend to operate with consistent processes, procedures, and expectations. When making the shift to creating an entrepreneurial culture, there needs to be an ongoing commitment to allow for innovations. Phrases like, "We have never done it like that before," or "We have always done it this way" are death sentences to an entrepreneurial culture. This is not to say the old way is not the best way, but an entrepreneurial culture encourages asking, "Are we sure there is not a better way?"

Even the existing structures within an organization can impede an entrepreneurial culture. For example, the workspace could inhibit the flow of creativity and innovation. Do employees have access to other employees, or do employees work in self-contained spaces or cubicles? Collaboration can lead to creation. Another structure that can impede entrepreneurial culture is management's openness to ideas. Organizations with a top-down approach will struggle more to encourage an entrepreneurial spirit in their employees. If employees don't have access to leadership, then neither do their ideas.

Solution

1. Companies: Review existing structures and policies to determine areas that may inhibit creativity. If workspaces keep employees independent, can they be restructured or can opportunities to gather and interact be added to operations? Be cognizant of thinking patterns that automatically reject new ideas or different approaches or are perceived to do so. When those thoughts arise, make a determination if there is space to consider the new idea or approach.

2. Organizations: We recommend organization provide their clients with a voice. Clients don't have to have a say in every aspect of the organization, but assess your programming to determine areas where:

   a. You could provide clients the opportunity to speak and bring new ideas.
   b. Your organization would benefit from new ideas.

   A social enterprise can be the space where women are given opportunities to be creative and entrepreneurial.

3. Women: Dream and dream big. If you were like some of the women in Shannon's study and stopped dreaming, it is time to start again. Ask yourself, "In a perfect world, what would I be doing now?" When you answer that question, you have the starting place of new adventures. From that starting place you can create a roadmap to fulfill that dream.

Challenges in Translation Factor

The primary challenge in this principle is judgment. The women in the stories discovered some of the skills they learned and used in their past could be translated to a professional work environment. That discovery required nonjudgmental acknowledgment and support from a trusted individual, who promoted the women's growth. Companies, nonprofit organizations, and women themselves have to work toward a nonjudgmental perspective about women's pasts and the skills and attributes they gained. Everyone can benefit from their past experiences.

Solution

1. Companies: Be cognizant of prejudices and not act on them when they arise. Start by realizing we all make mistakes. Some mistakes are more significant than others, but everyone wants to get past mistakes and move forward.

2. Organizations: Implement an asset-based approach to programming, if not already in place. Consider what skills, talents, and assets your clients bring to the table. Then take it a step farther

and assess what negative skills they used previously that can be applied in a new, healthy context.

3. Women: Don't let shame steal from you. You may have acted in ways you are not proud of or done things you wish you had not done, but it doesn't have to define or control you. Yes, there is no undoing the past. But you can move past the shame by taking accountability for past actions and redirecting your energy toward the pursuit of your dreams.

Challenges in Restorative Justice

There are two primary challenges that arise when adopting restorative practices. First, fully implementing restorative practices requires training. The second challenge is the paradigm shift. Restorative practices require us to look at everything we do through a different lens. This is particularly challenging in the early stages of implementation. For restorative practices to transform the organization, adoption should impact the culture and processes within your business.

Solution

1. Companies: The first solution would be to access restorative justice training. Most larger communities will have restorative justice practitioners providing training. There are also online courses teaching these principles. Another option is to create a restorative practices task force. This group would evaluate your current business environment for areas where restorative practices could enhance the current culture, processes, or activities.

2. Organizations: Assess current programming to determine where restorative practices like those mentioned in this book can be applied. Also explore the possibility of using restorative justice processes like circles. If working with the formerly incarcerated, explore programming to allow those individuals to take responsibility for past harms and make amends like we saw in several stories.

3. Women: As with the first two groups, take time to learn more about restorative justice. If you happen to be formerly incarcerated, consider whether you need to take greater responsibility for

harms you committed in the past. Incarceration is a form of paying a "debt," but as mentioned in chapter 5, its focus is on the law. Are their individuals or groups of individuals who were harmed by your actions that would welcome greater accountability from you?

Challenges in Partnerships

The first challenge in forging partnerships will be gaining mutual understanding of each other's missions and operations. Although nonprofit organizations and companies have some similarities, like staffing and administration, they are distinctly different. At their foundation, their primary missions are different; companies must generate a profit and nonprofit organizations must advance the public good. The two types of entities' operations differ in big and small ways as well. For example, companies rely on paid employees, whereas nonprofit organizations typically rely on a mix of paid employees and volunteers. This fundamental difference can impact the speed with which things happen and the values of the members involved.

Partnerships require organizations to learn each other's hidden rules and expectations about how things operate and how people interact. Not knowing the hidden rules or inherent culture of each entity can hinder effective partnerships between companies and nonprofit organizations.

Another challenge stems from a strength of business professionals. Often, they have learned to take charge and make things happen. Good business leaders assess situations, problems, or new ideas and quickly make changes to address those issues. Those strengths in business can hinder some of the approaches recommended in this book. As mentioned in chapter 6, all stakeholders in the partnership need to have an opportunity to provide input. At times business leaders must refrain from that quick response to allow input from both the nonprofit partner and the women being served.

A final challenge is for the women being served in the nonprofit. It can be overwhelming at first to work with business and nonprofit leaders. Every woman who presented a business plan to the Leadership Resource Team (LRT) in Cheryl's organization used language of fear or intimidation prior to the meeting.

Solution

1. Companies: Take time to learn or better understand the culture of the organization in the partnership. Ask leaders in the organization if there are hidden rules, that both employees and clients know are in place. If your company has significant values and approaches in relation to operations, take time to help the nonprofit leaders understand those values or approaches as well. Be cognizant of leaders' propensity to take charge. A business leader may be able to solve a problem more rapidly than one of the women like those in this book. However, there will be many times when it is far more advantageous to allow solutions to be discovered through input from the diverse perspectives in the partnership. Be especially encouraging to the women working with the nonprofit and give them an opportunity to be heard.

2. Organizations: Create materials that clearly detail your approach, philosophy, and culture to potential business partners. For example, in Cheryl's experience, it was important to train the LRT to use an asset-based approach. The women had unique skills and value they brought, which deserved to be acknowledged and considered when they were pitching business ideas. They were not in need or operating at a deficit. Further, the LRT needed to know the organization adopted an experiential learning model. Cheryl encouraged the LRT to pose questions that promoted more research and learning for the participants instead of simply telling them how to fix problems.

3. Women: Believe that you deserve a seat at the table. Nonprofit leaders and business leaders may look like they have it all together, but like everyone else, they have issues and real-life challenges. Although it may be intimidating, don't let it stop you. You have a perspective to offer that few people have. If you push through, you may very well be the one on the other side of the table helping women in the future.

We presented many challenges in this chapter. We hope you will focus more on the solutions than on the challenges. There is no challenge that is not worth overcoming to do the work of supporting women in their transformation. There is also not a problem that cannot be solved once you have involved the women receiving support. They have inventiveness and imagination in spades. As a reminder, in the appendix, there is an assessment your organization can take to determine areas where you are ready

> *There is no challenge that is not worth overcoming to do the work of supporting women in their transformation.*

to implement the principles and where more work needs to be done to minimize the challenges your organization might face in adopting each principle. We hope you will take the time to complete the assessment and consider where you are in this process.

⑧

RETHINKING STRUCTURES

Six women? *Hundreds* of women! Each woman—whose stories are woven together from hundreds of women we have met, to become Cara, Rosalinda, Emmie, Maggie, Diana, and Maria—is unique. But they share common experiences and gifts. They are resilient, brave, brilliant, and tough as nails when they need to be but gentle and loving as well. The women in these stories aren't projects needing help to overcome circumstance. They are survivors. They are overcomers.

So, what does all this mean for businesses? What can we learn from the six women's stories? Using the six guiding principles and the corresponding lessons learned from each woman, we can rethink current business structures that interfere with women who have been previously marginalized from being accepted in mainstream business environments. Yet the stories require us to rethink such structures as well as our own mindsets and biases. All too often, we go along seeing that things are not working but making wrong assumptions that lead to ineffective processes. We need, instead, to recognize that marginalized women, though often nontraditional employees, are incredible because of their life experiences and challenges and that their background is an asset on which companies can capitalize.

HIGH EXPECTATIONS FOR BUSINESSES

In every finance class, almost every business class—including the ones Shannon has taken and taught—the stated purpose of business is to increase shareholder wealth. The question business leaders are asking now is, "At what cost?" The public is demanding something different from business today than ever before. As consumers have grown in awareness of how business has often harmed workers, promoted inequality, devastated the natural world, and led to unjust outcomes, they are asking business to consider more than just profit by being mindful of people and planet. The idea may feel too mushy and unappealing if amassing great wealth is your only goal. However, if you are reading this book, we're guessing you are already looking for something more than just wealth. Maybe you are seeking impact and purpose. Business can be more: it can have a positive impact and a purpose that exceeds profits, while at the same time creating shareholder wealth.

The bottom line has expanded from only profit to the triple bottom line—people, planet, and profit. To focus on social and environmental improvements without considering profit, or even prioritizing profit, is not sustainable. In the same way, focusing on profit without consideration for social and environmental interests is not going to cut it anymore. Many investors and consumers just won't accept it. They are voting with their feet and their dollars and asking companies to be more and to do more.

The United Nations (UN) created the Sustainable Development Goals (SDGs), which were adopted by countries in 2015. The SDGs are intended to serve as a "blueprint for shared prosperity in a sustainable world—a world where all people can live productive, vibrant and peaceful lives on a healthy planet." Yes, please. The SDGs address seventeen major issues facing the world today. The agenda by 2030 is to make progress or eradicate big challenges facing the world today—zero hunger, clean water and sanitation, gender equality, quality education, and decent work and economic growth to name a few big goals. Do any of these initiatives touch your heart? Do any of these initiatives currently capture your dollars? You may already be investing in projects that will address these issues.

In 2013, the UN General Assembly established the Open Working Group, which developed the SDGs. The group developed a proposal for the SDGs using what the UN learned from the Millennium Development Goals (MDGs) adopted in 2000 with the goal to reduce poverty by 2015. In 2015, the General Assembly started negotiating the agenda developed by the Open Working Group with member countries. In 2015, all UN member countries adopted the 2030 Agenda for Sustainable Development, which included the seventeen SDGs. The creation and adoption were likely much easier than the implementation. Clearly, the seventeen goals are big goals. The SDGs expanded on the MDGs by expanding initiatives beyond developing countries to all countries and toward more ambitious and broad goals.

Measuring success has also been critical for the SDGs. The UN decided on 169 targets to measure countries' progress toward achieving the seventeen goals. Countries have made great progress since 2000. Yet, in the SDGs report from 2019, Antonio Guterres, the secretary general of the UN, said, "It is abundantly clear that a much deeper, faster and more ambitious response is needed to unleash the social and economic transformation needed to achieve our 2030 goals."[1]

The primary goal of this book aligns with SDG eight: "Promote sustained, inclusive and sustainable economic growth, full and productive employment and decent work for all."[2] We provide tools for creating sustainable economic growth and employment inclusive of women who have historically lived in the margins. Great progress has been made toward the targets associated with SDG eight, but great progress still needs to be made in overall gross domestic product (GDP), the gender pay gap, and disproportionately high unemployment for the young (three times higher than for adults). This book provides opportunities for companies to make a significant impact in these areas.

Also, important to this book is goal one: "End poverty in all its forms everywhere" as an example.[3] The target, which companies play a key role in achieving, is to eradicate extreme poverty, defined as living on less than $1.25 a day, by 2030.[4] The UN predicts we will fall short, with 6 percent of the world population remaining in extreme poverty in 2030, despite great improvements (36 percent in 1990 to 6 percent predicted in 2030).

Historically, we have relied on nonprofit organizations and the government to solve these problems, but realistically they cannot do it by themselves. The problems are too big. Business can help. In fact, many believe business is the only chance we have in bridging the gap left by nonprofit organizations and governments in creating significant, sustainable change in the areas identified in the SDGs.

In a robust review of studies investigating the correlation between sustainability, also called CSR, and economic performance, scholars found "companies with robust sustainability practices demonstrate better operational performance, which ultimately translates into cashflows."[5] CSR and profits do not have to be mutually exclusive or goals in conflict. As a business, you are best equipped to create sustainable change. Most nonprofit organizations do not think about the net present value (NPV) of their projects.

> CSR and profits do not have to be mutually exclusive or goals in conflict.

A PROFITABLE AND IMPACTFUL INVESTMENT

Investing in women is a positive NPV project for businesses and society. As we mentioned in the introduction, making investments is powerful because of the multiplier effect. Investing in women benefits the whole family because the money a woman makes is typically spent directly on benefiting her family. When a woman is elevated, she can make a significant contribution to her family's health, education, and well-being. Such an investment has the power to impact societies across the world and families in your city. According to the Women in Work Index 2018, if other countries increased women's employment rates consistent with those of Sweden, the GDP worldwide could increase by more than $6 trillion.[6]

Further, numerous studies show a significant impact on profitability when companies have gender diversity. In 2018, McKinsey & Company reported companies in the top quartile for gender diversity were 21 percent "more likely to experience above-average profitability than companies in the fourth quartile."[7] The International Labour Organization illustrated the impact of women's representation in corporations with increased profits, in addition to improved "productivity; increased ability to attract and retain talent; greater creativity, innovation and openness; enhanced reputation; and the ability to better gauge consumer interest and demand."[8] Gender diversity brings unique perspectives into business and leads to long-term profitability.

The women in these stories brought powerfully unique perspectives to the companies they led and owned. They uplifted organizations and communities. We are convinced hiring women, especially women like those in these six stories, will have an incredibly positive impact on companies and the world. We are also not naïve enough to think it is easy or without challenges.

REVISITING THE SIX PRINCIPLES

Let's review the six principles that emerged from the stories of the women.

1. Experiential or discovery learning model is an approach that allows for the discovery of new information, as opposed to the traditional dissemination of new information.
2. Immediate leadership opportunities allow employees the opportunity to lead in a safe setting that accepts mistakes as a part of the process.
3. Entrepreneurial culture is intentionally creating and cultivating a culture that focuses on innovation and efficiency as a priority.
4. Translation factor is the realization that employees can translate skills, attributes, and strategies, even those gained through nontraditional experiences, into other contexts with productive results. It also is used when skills from one context are transferred to another.
5. Restorative justice principles of direct voice, safe place, value-based, stakeholder focus, and accountability are concepts organizations can weave into the culture of any organization.

6. Nonprofit partnerships become an effective tool for insight into nontraditional employees, as well as a launching or training ground for potentially new employees.

The information in each woman's story details an individual guiding principle. But it is important to synthesize and categorize the principles to make connections within your organization.

Which principles are paradigm shifts? Which principles are more action-oriented? Which require program development? Which principles are concept driven? To make it easier to determine a starting point, we put the principles into four categories: program-oriented, concept driven, action-oriented, and paradigm shifts. All of the six principles will fall into one or two categories seen in figure 8.1.

The categories are helpful because they identify what drives the action for implementation. For instance, translation factor requires us to shift how we view people, assets, and experiences. However, it is also action-oriented, meaning once that shift is made, we begin to translate experience into different contexts. This can be in the form of skills from the past, like seen in Maggie's story. It can be translating programs developed in a nonprofit setting into a business setting or vice-versa. The Next Steps section later in this chapter will provide concrete examples of how to implement these principles based on these categories.

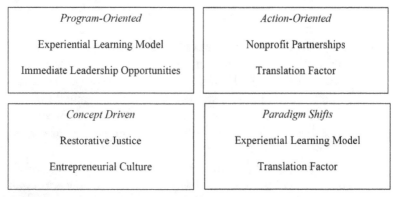

Program-Oriented	*Action-Oriented*
Experiential Learning Model	Nonprofit Partnerships
Immediate Leadership Opportunities	Translation Factor
Concept Driven	*Paradigm Shifts*
Restorative Justice	Experiential Learning Model
Entrepreneurial Culture	Translation Factor

Figure 8.I.   Principle categorization.

Program-oriented principles will require businesses to develop and implement programs based on the concepts. For instance, experiential learning can become a program offered through continuing professional development or continuing education requirements already in place within companies; more details are in the Next Steps section. The implementation for this would either be modifying the existing requirements or programs creating it if it does not already exist.

Action-oriented principles will require a tangible action to occur like research or connections forged. Concept-driven principles will require learning or training prior to implementation. This can be in the form of training for employees or management. It can be through providing resources for learning like articles or books based on the concepts. Paradigm-shift principles will require an intentional shifting of business leaders, view of their business and employees.

Further, let us explore the interrelationship of the principles working together as a whole. Even though we highlighted one principle in each story, you may have already identified overlap between the principles. For example, both immediate leadership opportunities and experiential learning rely heavily on project-based learning and learning by doing. Further, organizations can use experiential learning to support innovation central to an entrepreneurial culture.

Most importantly, when looking at how these principles intersect, something interesting emerges. All of the principles work together to create an environment ripe for restorative justice. We have found business leaders, at times, to be skeptical about the value of or need to implement restorative justice. Yet, restorative justice creates a central connection to the other principles. When working with individuals who have experienced marginalization or trauma, adopting a culture conducive with restorative practices is critical. For example, when restorative justice elements permeate an organization, it creates a safe place for individuals to learn and fall forward through experiential or discovery learning, immediate leadership opportunities, and an entrepreneurial culture. The drive for innovation and growth outweighs the shame and disappointment that can come from failure. At the same time, as a critical element of restorative justice, accountability holds employees to a high standard to acknowledge and then learn from their mistakes.

Translation factor interacts with restorative justice through the encouragement of survivors of challenging situations to acknowledge and validate the skills they gained through past experiences, even non-traditional experiences. The interaction of restorative justice with the other principles recognizes the opportunity for failure and the need to own that failure as a part of the learning. Using a direct voice, or compassionate confrontation, allows managers to provide clear communication about the expectations they have for employees and work with employees when those expectations are not met related to the other principles.

Focusing on implementing one principle at a time can be helpful in transforming an organization's culture, policies, and practices to align with the six principles. The goal, however, is for the principles to eventually translate into the standard modus operandi of your business. When all these elements overlap and work cohesively as a whole, catalytic rapid transformation occurs. Getting to the place of all the individual elements working as one will take intentionality and time.

NEXT STEPS TOWARD IMPLEMENTATION

There are two primary approaches businesses can take for implementation of the six principles—internally developing programming needed to implement the principles or outsourcing such programming through partnerships with other organizations.

Internal Program Development

There are extensive opportunities for implementing the six principles through internal program development. Many ideas may come from each chapter. We explicitly outline two here, as examples—revamping continuing education to incorporate experiences and expanding development and cross-training programs to all levels in the organization.

Continuing education is a potentially effective space for implementing experiential learning. Many companies require ongoing training. Many professional organizations require members to invest time in continuing education through credentialing, continuing professional education (CPE), continuing education units (CEUs), and the like. Most people meet their continuing education requirements by attending conferences, seminars, or webinars. Although those activities can be highly beneficial by exposing employees or professionals to new trends or innovations in the industry, they typically do not require learning by doing.

Alternatively, companies and professional organizations could create opportunities for continued education using experiential learning initiatives. Women who interned through the housing program created projects for the organization, much like a capstone project in business school. The only parameters for the project were to benefit the social enterprise directly. Once the intern developed and submitted the project, the staff reviewed it for viability. Then, the intern would transition to implementing the idea.

This process created two amazing outcomes. First, the women were free to pursue topics that were of interest and became highly motivated to work on their project. They would get so excited that they would have to be reminded they had other work that still needed to be accomplished. This created the need to learn time management. They had tasks that were expected of them, and they had a project they were eager to develop, and both had to be balanced and prioritized.

The second benefit of this approach was the unexpected increase of programming. When this started, there were minimal expectations of the impact of the projects. The intern projects existed solely to create an experiential learning lab of sorts. No one expected the profound results of that method. The women came up with innovative new processes, new programs, and new opportunities. After a few years, most of the programming that was done at the social enterprise had been developed as intern projects. Imagine what that could mean for businesses. What if continuing education requirements could be met by allowing employees to create a project to positively impact the company's bottom line. The employees could develop a project for consideration with the only parameter being that it had to benefit the organization.

Further, the six principles can be incorporated into training programs for new hires based on the six principles. For example, related to immediate leadership opportunities, many companies have cross-training and development programs at the corporate level, but these opportunities do not permeate all positions across the company. If internal implementation is not realistic in executing some or all of the principles, then partnerships can create opportunities to outsource implementation.

Outsourcing through Partnerships

Outsourcing through partnerships with nonprofits and for-profit organizations could also be fruitful in training and screening potential employees with less traditional backgrounds. We dedicated a chapter to nonprofit partnerships, but it is worth further exploring here. Partnerships with nonprofit and even other for-profit organizations can create a pipeline for talent into your organization. Nonprofit organizations, especially those with a social enterprise, are well-prepared to implement the six principles in training participants for future work. This was the method for the Texas housing program Cheryl ran. Women in Cheryl's program learned many new skills and learned to translate old skills into business through the organization's social enterprise.

Other businesses can play a similar role by helping provide a training ground or pipeline for potential employees coming that are a good fit for your organization. For example, an employee can work at a call center prior to working in a remote office for a corporation and then the corporate office. The pipeline provides opportunities for employees to grow and develop and for the company to determine if they are a fit for future positions. Call centers were starting points for many women in the housing program and for at least one participant in Shannon's study. The participant described learning basic employable skills, like typing, gained exposure to a highly structured work environment, and gained customer service experience. Many women worked in restaurants. Collaborating with a restaurant or other company with aligned skills to positions you are working to fill could be an effective strategy. Finding an entry-level position, even if it is outside of your company, from which you can recruit, could be valuable.

Which approach you take—internal program development or outsourcing through partnerships—might depend on how ready your company is currently to implement the six principles. In the appendix, we have provided an assessment tool you can use to determine your organization's readiness.

A PROMISING FUTURE AND SUCCESSFUL STORIES

Many companies are rethinking hiring policies to consider individuals who were previously incarcerated.[9] The transformation in hiring would have been unprecedented just a few years ago. However, with increased competition for employees, many companies are working toward at least giving formerly incarcerated individuals the same chance to secure a job as anyone else. The White House has worked on this seemingly nonpartisan issue, starting with the Fair Chance Business Pledge adopted in 2016.[10] Companies like American Airlines, the Coca-Cola Company, Facebook, Google, the Hershey Company, PepsiCo, Starbucks, Under Amour, Unilever, Xerox, and many more signed the pledge. By doing so, they committed to reducing barriers for formerly incarcerated individuals to gain employment, when they are qualified. Reducing barriers includes pushing criminal history questions and background checks to later in the hiring process. The hope behind the pledge was for employers to consider applicant's criminal record in proper context, rather than immediately dismissing an individual.

Several companies have already been successful hiring formerly incarcerated individuals. One example is Greyston Bakery in New York, which signed the pledge but is years ahead of many of the other companies to sign. Greyston Bakery practices "open hiring," which they have done for more than thirty years. Now sixty-five of their workforce includes people who were formerly incarcerated.

Similarly, Televerde, a company running call centers for technology companies like Microsoft, Dell, and Adobe, hires women while they are still in prison and considers them for open full-time positions after release. In 2018, the company employed fifty-eight women who are former inmates at their Phoenix location, who earn an average base salary of slightly more than fifty-two thousand dollars.[11] Formerly incarcerated women work at all levels, including the executive level, for Televerde.

ADDITIONAL RESOURCES

In the appendix, you will find several tools to use in implementing the principles in this book, including a readiness assessment. The readiness assessment is a diagnostic tool to help you evaluate your organization's current ability to benefit from women like Cara, Rosalinda, Emmie, Maggie, Diana, and Maria. Multiple people in your organization should complete the assessment and compare results to mitigate any blind spots any one employee might have about your organization's readiness.

If you determined through the assessment tool that your organization is not fully prepared to make an impact in women's lives like those in this book, then there are additional resources that can better prepare you for the process. An excellent resource to gain greater understanding of poverty and effective approaches is the book *When Helping Hurts: How to Alleviate Poverty Without Hurting the Poor . . . and Yourself* by Steve Corbett and Brian Fikkert.[12]

There are many resources available to learn about restorative justice. *Changing Lenses: Restorative Justice for Our Times* by Howard Zehr is an excellent book that helped initiate the restorative justice movement in the United States.[13] Keep in mind, restorative justice has its roots in the criminal justice field, so when reading Zehr's book remember the translation factor and evaluate the principles from a business perspective. There are also numerous opportunities to be trained in restorative justice. Cheryl provides training to businesses seeking to learn introductory principles of restorative justice. She has also published a book, *Language of Shalom: 7 Keys to Practical Reconciliation*, that addresses restorative justice from a community context.[14] Eastern Mennonite University provides summer institute training on a variety of restorative justice concepts, processes, and practices.

A wide variety of resources are available through books and media on how to create an entrepreneurial culture in your workplace. One resource is *Entrepreneurial Life: The Path From Startup to Market Leader* by Bob Luddy.[15]

IN CLOSING . . .

> If a man has a hundred sheep, and one wanders away and is lost, what will he do? Won't he leave the ninety-nine others and go out into the hills to search for the lost one? And if he finds it, he will rejoice over it more than over the ninety-nine others safe at home!
>
> Matt. 18:12–14

In business, we have set about to make profit and products and provide good and sustainable lives for ourselves and our employees. Even if you don't ascribe to the Christian faith, the passage creates an interesting image or dilemma. As business leaders, do we care about the one who wandered off and was lost? If so, then we are called to the margins to search for those who found themselves in dark and lonely spaces. Historically, society has left the work of finding the lost and lonely to the church and nonprofits. But we have built a case that we need socially responsible businesses to fill the gap.

So, here's to all the business owners who want to make a difference. And cheers to all managers and businesses who see potential in everyone and benefiting greatly for it. The result can bring you fulfillment and can bring growth to your business.

And here's to all the women like Cara, Rosalinda, Emmie, Maggie, Diana, and Maria out there: You are strong. Push through. A future you cannot imagine today is waiting for you. And the world needs you!

APPENDIX

The additional documents in this appendix include a readiness assessment that companies and nonprofit organizations can use to determine how prepared they are currently to hire women who are overcoming challenging pasts. The documents that follow are planning documents that companies, nonprofit organization, and women overcoming challenging pasts can use to get more prepared to implement the principles in this book.

Finally, we provide some active listening tools that can be used during difficult dialogues. Specifically, these active-listening tools can make implementing the requirements of restorative justice more effective. Active listening is one of the most important aspects of communication.

READINESS ASSESSMENT

The readiness assessment is a diagnostic tool to help you evaluate your organization's current ability to benefit from Cara, Rosalinda, Emmie, Maggie, Diana, and Maria. Multiple people in your organization should complete the assessment and compare results to mitigate any blind spots any employee might have about your organization's readiness.

Assessment Instructions: Assign each numbered statement with a rating from the scale provided. The purpose is to answer how well each statement fits your organization.

3 = Almost always; 2 = Occasionally; 1 = Almost never

1. We consider all individuals impacted by our decisions and actions. ___
2. We have a development program, such as a rotational program or leadership development program, for all employees and not just those in corporate office positions. ___
3. We value talent development enough to invest in raw talent that might require coaching and encouragement to develop. ___
4. Our workplace promotes feedback and suggestions. ___
5. We pay a living wage to all employees, including those in entry-level positions. ___
6. We have positions that provide opportunities for growth for individuals who join the company at all levels. ___
7. Our organization invests in community development projects aligned with our company's strategic mission. ___
8. Personal responsibility is an important value in our company. ___
9. Supervisors are accepting and encouraging of employees who make a mistake or asks questions the first time they are completing a new task. ___
10. Our organization allows employees to work through stretch projects, even when it takes longer, to reap the longer-term benefits from employee development. ___
11. Our organization values and rewards innovative ideas from employees at all levels. ___
12. Our organization uses personality assessments like Clifton-Strengths, Birkman, Myers-Briggs, or others to discover employees' talents and strengths that align with the company's strategy. ___
13. Supervisors delegate new tasks to their employees, without micromanaging, even when the supervisor knows it will take them longer to learn by doing. ___

14. Managers in the organization provide rewards and recognition when employees present innovative ideas. ___

15. We have clear advancement pipelines within our organization, so all employees can see future opportunities for promotion. ___

16. We have partnerships with nonprofit organizations in the community that help meet our hiring needs. ___

17. We have partnerships with organizations that can meet our employees' needs, such as childcare. ___

18. Our organization is entrepreneurial enough to change policies and practices within our organization to make a difference. ___

19. Employees' engagement is high in optional workplace activities (willingness, safe place). ___

20. Our workplace recognizes and embraces different perspectives and values of all employees. ___

21. We allow employees to take the lead on a variety of projects. ___

22. We provide new employees with early opportunities to lead a task or project. ___

23. Supervisors in our company receive formal training on mentoring and coaching employees, especially employees with diverse experiences and perspectives. ___

24. Our company will consider hiring qualified individuals with criminal records. ___

25. Employees have access to resources to learn new tasks independently. ___

26. Supervisors are trained in how to support employees' learning through experiences. ___

27. Our organization is always evaluating existing processes, products, and work activities. ___

28. Our organization allows employees time to research competitors and other processes. ___

29. Our company's focus is on long-term community impact and transformation. ___

30. Our company knows the values and expectations of our nonprofit partners. ___

Scoring Instructions: Combine your scores from the previous statements in the categories given in the scoring table.

Principle 1: Experiential Learning	Principle 2: Immediate Leadership Opportunities	Principle 3: Entrepreneurial Culture	Principle 4: Translation Factor	Principle 5: Restorative Justice	Principle 6: Nonprofit Partnership
Item 9: ___	Item 2: ___	Item 11: ___	Item 3: ___	Item 1: ___	Item 7: ___
Item 10: ___	Item 6: ___	Item 14: ___	Item 5: ___	Item 4: ___	Item 16: ___
Item 13: ___	Item 15: ___	Item 18: ___	Item 12: ___	Item 8: ___	Item 17: ___
Item 25: ___	Item 21: ___	Item 27: ___	Item 23: ___	Item 19: ___	Item 29: ___
Item 26: ___	Item 22: ___	Item 28: ___	Item 24: ___	Item 20: ___	Item 30: ___
Total: ___	Total: ___	Total: ___	Total: ___	Total: ___	Total: ___

Grand total: ___

Individual principle score interpretation: A score of 13 to 15 for any principle indicates your organization is currently thriving in the implementation of that principle.

A score of 9 to 12 for any principle may indicate concern regarding your organization's ability to implement that principle.

A score of 5 to 8 for any principle indicates policies and practices within your organizations need to be adjusted to effectively implement the principle.

Overall score interpretation: Because the principles are interrelated, we recommend evaluating your overall score. If your organization scored between 72 and 90 points, your organization is likely ready to benefit from hiring women like those in this book. Continue to monitor the policies and practices within your company to ensure that, at a minimum, your organization maintains the current status.

If your organization scored between 51 and 71 points, then leadership needs to do additional work to prepare for providing a positive professional environment for women like those in this book. If you scored within this range but answered 3 to question 18, then you are likely ready. If your organization does not adapt quickly, then implementing the principles and strategies in this book would be more difficult.

If your organization scored between 30 and 51 points, then the principles and strategies in this book might not be a good fit at this time. The organization would need to go through dramatic changes to successfully implement the principles. If you don't have the influence within your organization to make such changes and you are passionate about the outcomes in this book, then you might consider moving to a different organization. You can use this assessment to screen other organizations with employment opportunities aligned with your goals.

PLANNING DOCUMENTS

Use the following document that corresponds to your role—as a company, a nonprofit organization, or a woman overcoming a challenging past.

Next Steps: Planning for Companies

Step 1. Complete the readiness assessment.
Step 2. Identify stakeholders—identify a team of stakeholders who need to be involved in plans to implement the six principles in this book. Ensure you include employees who have overcome challenging pasts in the planning.
    a. List team members
Step 3. Strengthening your organization.
    a. Looking back at your readiness assessment, which principles, or elements within a principle, does your company already use effectively?
        i.
        ii.
        iii.
    b. Do any of these areas, where you use the principles or elements effectively, need to be developed to a greater capacity? If so, how?
    Area to improve:
    How:
    What resources are needed:
Step 4. Identifying weaknesses: Looking back at the readiness assessment, which principles are not currently being used effectively.?
    a. Which principle, or element of a principle, needs to be addressed first?
        i. Resources needed:
        ii. Steps to implement this element in our company:
        iii. Barriers in implementation:
        iv. Methods for addressing each barrier:
    b. Which principle, or element of a principle, needs to be addressed next?
        i. Resources needed:
        ii. Steps to implement this element in our company:
        iii. Barriers in implementation:
        iv. Methods for addressing each barrier:

      c. Which principle, or element of a principle, needs to be addressed next?
          i. Resources needed:
          ii. Steps to implement this element in our company:
          iii. Barriers in implementation:
          iv. Methods for addressing each barrier:

Step 5. List current nonprofits collaborations.

Step 6. List new potential nonprofit collaborations.

Next Steps: Planning for Nonprofit Organizations

Step 1. Complete the readiness assessment.

Step 2. Identify stakeholders—Create a team of stakeholders for your nonprofit organization, including board, key staff, decision-makers, and most importantly, clients served.
      a. List team members

Step 3. Strengthening your organization.
      a. Looking back at your readiness assessment, which principles, or elements within a principle, are already being used effectively?
          i.
          ii.
          iii.
      b. Do any of these areas, where you use the principles or elements effectively, need to be developed to a greater capacity? If so, how?
      Area(s) to improve:
      How:
      What resources are needed:

Step 4. Identifying weaknesses: Looking back at the readiness assessment, which principles are not currently being used effectively?
      a. Which principle, or element of a principle, needs to be addressed first?
          i. Resources needed:
          ii. Steps to implement this element in our company:

       iii. Barriers in implementation:

       iv. Methods for addressing each barrier:

   b. Which principle, or element of a principle, needs to be addressed next?

       i. Resources needed:

       ii. Steps to implement this element in our company:

       iii. Barriers in implementation:

       iv. Methods for addressing each barrier:

   c. Which principle, or element of a principle, needs to be addressed next?

       i. Resources needed:

       ii. Steps to implement this element in our company:

       iii. Barriers in implementation:

       iv. Methods for addressing each barrier:

Step 5. List current business partners, partnerships, and collaborations.

Step 6. List new business partners, partnerships, and collaborations.

Next Step Planning for Women

Step 1. Set goals that you have for yourself after reading this book. Remember to dream big!!!

   Goal 1

   Goal 2

   Goal 3

   Goal 4

Step 2. Identify stakeholders—Who do I need on my team to help me reach my goals?

   a. List team members

Step 3. Complete the following behavior and thinking assessment.

   a. List your five most destructive behaviors.

       i.

       ii.

       iii.

       iv.

       v.

Step 4. Living in a destructive lifestyle rarely happens in a vacuum. Sometimes those who are closest to us say the most hurtful

words about our choices and actions. List some of the negative
things that others have said about you.

    i.

    ii.

    iii.

Step 5. Reapplying skills.

    a. Looking at the previous list, can any of those actions or
behaviors be translated and applied to healthy, productive
activities? If so how? You may need to seek the help of your
team on this section.

Step 6. Analyzing thinking errors.

    a. What thinking errors, like those listed in chapter 5, have
you used in the past (i.e., blaming others, justifying actions,
making excuses, making assumptions)?

        i.

        ii.

        iii.

        iv.

        v.

    b. How will you address each error and seek to stop using
them?

        i.

        ii.

        iii.

        iv.

        v.

Step 7. Assessing your past failures.

    a. List the three most significant times you failed in your life.

        i.

        ii.

        iii.

    b. What were personal factors that lead to those failures?

        i.

        ii.

        iii.

    c. Were there any external factors that contributed to the
failure?

      i.

      ii.

      iii.

d. Did anything change after each failure?

      i.

      ii.

      iii.

e. Can or did you modify any of the personal and external factors? If so, how?

f. What if anything did you learn from these failures?

g. What have you learned in this exercise or in this book that you can use to help you attain your goals?

ACTIVE LISTENING TOOLS

Active listening is a critical aspect of communication. For the restorative justice principles discussed in chapter 5 to be most effective, all stakeholders need to engage in active listening. The following tools can help you become a better active listener.

Active Listening Dos and Don'ts

The following strategies are based on the HURIER model.[1] In the acronym, H stands for hearing, U stands for understanding, R stands for remembering, I stands for interpreting, E stands for evaluating, and the last R stands for responding.

To implement the HURIER model as a listener you should:

- Prior to the conversation, recognize how your previous experiences may impact your interpretation of the conversation.
- Minimize distractions and disruptions.
- Listen for understanding, trying to imagine the needs, feeling, and values associated with the message.
- Work to put yourself in the other person's place. Try to look at the situation from his or her position.
- Ask questions to clarify meaning or unfamiliar vocabulary.

- Implement memory techniques, including note-taking, to increase recall.
- Watch for nonverbal cues.
- Recognize the emotional tones in the speaker's message.
- Evaluate your emotions and biases in an effort to maintain objectivity.
- Listen to the speaker's points in entirety before responding.
- Restate important thoughts and feelings expressed by the speaker as you continue to listen.
- Respond carefully, being mindful of your emotions, tone, and nonverbal cues.

To implement the HURIER model as a listener you should not:

- Interrupt.
- Plan what you are going to say next. Listening is not preparing for how you will respond to what is being said. When you begin to think about how you want to respond, you stop listening and can process messages inaccurately.
- Provide advice. So many times, when we hear messages about conflict or harm, an instinct of wanting to provide advice kicks in. Giving advice is an excellent tool in some contexts but not in active listening.
- Try to relate to the speaker by sharing your own experiences. Although, wanting to connect over a shared experience is a common reaction to hearing a difficult message, avoid the urge to bring up similar problems from your own experience. Using phrases like "I understand" can backfire.

NOTES

INTRODUCTION

1. "Welcome to the #GirlCollective," *Dove.com*, accessed October 20, 2020, from: https://www.dove.com/us/en/stories/campaigns/girl-collective .html.

2. Shannon Deer and Jill Zarestky, "Balancing Profit and People: Corporate Social Responsibility in Business Education," *Journal of Management Education* 41, no. 5 (2017), 728, doi: 10.1177/1052562917719918.

3. "2019 Health for Humanity Report: Progress in Sustainability," Johnson & Johnson, accessed October 20, 2020, from: https://healthforhumanity report.jnj.com/_document/2019-heath-for-humanity-report-johnson-johnson ?id=00000172-a8f8-dff3-a9fa-acfda52c0000.

4. "Google Environmental Report 2019," *Google*, accessed October 20, 2020, from: https://sustainability.google/reports/environmental-report-2019/.

5. Ana Angelovksa, "Reshaping Reputation in the Workplace," *RepTrak*, July 22, 2019, accessed from: https://www.reptrak.com/blog/reshaping -reputation-in-the-workplace/.

6. Mary Pflum, "As Millennial Parents Demand Sustainable Toys, Lego Is Perfecting Plant-Based Bricks," *NBC News*, August 2, 2019, accessed from: https://www.nbcnews.com/business/consumer/millennial-parents-demand -sustainable-toys-lego-perfecting-plant-based-bricks-n1038721.

7. David Brooks, *The Second Mountain: The Quest for a Moral Life* (London, United Kingdom: Penguin, 2019).

8. Clarice A. Auluck-Wilson, "When All Women Lift," *Signs*, Summer (1995): 1032, https://www.jstor.org/stable/3174894.

9. John Hoddinott and Lawrence Haddad, "Does Female Income Share Influence Household Expenditures? Evidence from Côte D'Ivoire," *Oxford Bulletin of Economics and Statistics* 57, no. 1 (1995): 94, doi: 10.1111/j.1468 -0084.1995.tb00028.x.

10. David E. Bloom, Michael Kuhn, and Klaus Prettner, "Invest in Women and Prosper," *Finance and Development* 54, no. 3 (2017): 1, https://www.imf.org/external/pubs/ft/fandd/2017/09/bloom.htm.

11. Melinda Gates, *The Moment of Lift: How Empowering Women Changes the World* (New York: Flatiron Books, 2019), 28.

12. Gates, *The Moment of Lift*, 53.

13. The study referenced here and throughout this book was approved by the Institutional Review Board (IRB) at Texas A&M University. An IRB's mission is to protect human participants recruited for research studies. The research was conducted by Shannon Deer, after IRB approval. The study has been published in several peer-reviewed journal articles, which are cited as applicable. In other publications, participants were given a pseudonym. No participant names or pseudonyms were used in this book. Their stories along with other women Cheryl supported inspired the stories in this book. Analysis of their experiences led to the findings that support the principles as stated throughout the book.

CHAPTER I

1. Susan A. Ambrose, Michael W. Bridges, Michele DiPietro, Marsha C. Lovett, and Marie K. Norman, *How Learning Works: Seven Research-Based Principles for Smart Teaching* (San Francisco: Jossey-Bass, 2010).

2. Sharan B. Merriam and Laura L. Bierema, *Adult Learning: Linking Theory and Practice* (San Francisco: Jossey-Bass, 2013).

3. Ambrose et al., *How Learning Works*.

4. Ambrose et al., *How Learning Works*.

5. David A. Kolb, *Experiential Learning: Experience as the Source of Learning and Development* (Upper Saddle River, NJ: Pearson Education, 2015).

6. Kolb, *Experiential Learning*.

7. Merriam and Bierema, *Adult Learning*.

8. Mel Silberman, *The Handbook of Experiential Learning* (San Francisco: Pfeiffer, 2007).

9. Shannon Deer, Jill Zarestky, and Lisa M. Baumgartner, "'Learn How to Hustle for Good': Women's Work Transitions out of the Sex Trade," *Human Resource Development* 31, no. 1 (2019), doi: 10.1002/hrdq.21382.

10. Deer, Zarestky, and Baumgartner, "'Learn How to Hustle for Good,'" 41.

11. Deer, Zarestky, and Baumgartner, "'Learn How to Hustle for Good,'" 41.

12. John Dewey, *Experience and Education* (New York: Collier Books, 1963).

13. Lev S. Vygotsky, *Mind in Society* (Cambridge, MA: Harvard University Press, 1978).

14. James Balagot, "Inside Learning: How Yelp Created a Successful Learning Culture," *Continu*, September 1, 2017, available at: https://blog.continu.co/yelp-successful-learning-culture/.

15. Balagot, "Inside Learning."

16. Ambrose et al., *How Learning Works.*

CHAPTER 2

1. Shannon Deer and Lisa Baumgartner, "'I Can Relate': Survivor Leadership Supporting Women Transitioning out of the Sex Trade," *Adult Learning* 30, no. 4 (2019), available at: https://search.ebscohost.com/login.aspx?direct=true&db=eric&AN=EJ1231274&site=eds-live.

2. Deer and Baumgartner, "'I Can Relate,'" 170.

3. Deer and Baumgartner, "'I Can Relate,'" 170.

4. Deer and Baumgartner, "'I Can Relate,'" 169.

5. Deer and Baumgartner, "'I Can Relate,'" 171.

6. Deer and Baumgartner, "'I Can Relate,'" 169.

7. Deer and Baumgartner, "'I Can Relate,'" 170.

8. Deer and Baumgartner, "'I Can Relate.'"

9. Ellen A. Ensher, Craig Thomas, and Susan E. Murphy, "Comparison of Transitional Step-Ahead, and Peer Mentoring on Protégés' Support, Satisfaction, and Perceptions of Career Success: A Social Exchange Perspective," *Journal of Business and Psychology* 15, no. 3 (2001): 419–38, doi: 10.1023/A:1007870600459.

10. Norma Hotaling, Autumn Burris, B. Julie Johnson, Yoshi M. Bird, and Kirsten A. Melbye, "Been There Done That: SAGE, A Peer Leadership Model among Prostitution Survivors," *Journal of Trauma Practice* 2 (2003): 255–65. doi:10.1300/J189v02n03_15.

11. Hotaling et al., "Been There Done That," 260.

12. Hotaling et al., "Been There Done That," 259.

13. Deer and Baumgartner, "'I Can Relate.'"

14. Djoerd Hiemstra and Nico W. Van Yperen, "The Effects of Strength-Based Versus Deficit-Based Self-Regulated Learning Strategies on Students' Effort Intentions," *Motivation and Emotions* 39 (2015): 656–68, https://doi.org/10.1007/s11031-015-9488-8. Mary O'Hagan, "Leadership for Empowerment and Equality: A Proposed Model for Mental Health User/Survivor Leadership," *The International Journal of Leadership in Public Services* 5, no. 4 (2009): 34–43, doi:10.5042/ijlps.2010.0110.

15. O'Hagan, "Leadership for Empowerment and Equality," 40.

16. Rebecca J. Macy and Natalie Johns, "Aftercare Services for International Sex Trafficking Survivors: Informing U.S. Service and Program Development in an Emerging Practice Area," *Trauma, Violence, and Abuse* 12, no. 2 (2011): 92, doi:10.1177/1524838010390709.

17. Hotaling et al., "Been There Done That," 263.

18. Cooperrider Center, "Why Appreciative Inquiry?" Champlain College, accessed October 25, 2020, from: https://www.champlain.edu/ai-home/what-is-appreciative-inquiry/why-appreciative-inquiry.

19. Cooperrider Center, "Who Uses Appreciative Inquiry?" Champlain College, accessed October 25, 2020, from: https://www.champlain.edu/ai-home/what-is-appreciative-inquiry/who-uses-appreciative-inquiry.

CHAPTER 3

1. Gifford Pinchot III, "Four Definitions for the Intrapreneur," *The Pinchot Perspective*, October 30, 2017, accessed from: https://www.pinchot.com/2017/10/four-definitions-for-the-intrapreneur.html.

2. Gifford Pinchot III and Elizabeth S. Pinchot, "Intra-Corporate Entrepreneurship," Fall 1978, accessed from: https://drive.google.com/file/d/0B6GgwqtG-DKcSlpsbGRBZkZYSlk/view.

3. Peter B. Robinson, David V. Stimpson, Jonathan C. Huefner, and H. Keith Hunt, "An Attitude Approach to the Prediction of Entrepreneurship," *Entrepreneurship: Theory and Practice* 15 (1991): 13–32, https://www.researchgate.net/profile/Jonathan_Huefner/publication/270820261_An_Attitude_Approach_to_the_Prediction_of_Entrepreneurship/links/55ef024008aedecb68fd8f02.pdf.

4. Jose Carlos Pinho and Elisabete Sampaio de Sá, "Personal Characteristics, Business Relationships and Entrepreneurial Performance: Some

Empirical Evidence," *Journal of Small Business and Enterprise Development* 21, no. 2 (2014): 284–300.

   5. Deer, Zarestky, and Baumgartner, "'Learn How to Hustle for Good,'" 39.

   6. James C. Hayton and Gabriella Cacciotti, "Is There an Entrepreneurial Culture? A Review of Empirical Research," *Entrepreneurship and Regional Development* 25, nos. 9–10 (2013): 708–31, http://dx.doi.org/10.1080/0 8985626.2013.862962. Carla S. Marques, Sandra Valente, and Marisa Lages, "The Influence of Personal and Organisational Factors on Entrepreneurship Intention: An Application in the Health Care Sector," *Journal of Nursing Management* 26 (2018): 696–706. Pinho and Sampaio de Sá, "Personal Characteristics, Business Relationships and Entrepreneurial Performance."

   7. Hayton and Cacciotti, "Is There an Entrepreneurial Culture?"

   8. Margaret J. Wheatley, *Turning to One Another: Simple Conversations to Restore Hope to the Future* (San Francisco: Berrett-Koshler Publishers, Inc., 2002), 38–40.

   9. Pinho and Sampaio de Sá, "Personal Characteristics, Business Relationships and Entrepreneurial Performance."

   10. Hermann Brandstätter, "Personality Aspect of Entrepreneurship: A Look at Five Meta-Analyses," *Personality and Individual Differences* 51, no. 3 (2011): 222–30. Andreas Rauch and Michael Frese, "Let's Put the Person Back into Entrepreneurship Research: A Meta-Analysis on the Relationship between Business Owners' Personality Traits, Business Creation, and Success," *European Journal of Work and Organizational Psychology* 16, no. 4 (2007): 353–85. Scott Shane and Nicos Nicolaou, "Creative Personality, Opportunity Recognition and the Tendency to Start Businesses: A Study of Their Genetic Predispositions," *Journal of Business Ventures* 30, no. 3 (2015): 407–19.

   11. United Nations, "The Sustainable Development Goals Report 2019," *UnitedNations.com*, 11, accessed from: https://unstats.un.org/sdgs/report/2019/.

   12. Pinho and Sampaio de Sá, "Personal Characteristics, Business Relationships and Entrepreneurial Performance."

   13. Nancy Folbre, *The Invisible Heart: Economics and Family Values* (New York: New Press, 2002).

   14. Auluck-Wilson, "When All Women Lift," 1038.

CHAPTER 4

   1. Deer, Zarestky, and Baumgartner, "'Learn How to Hustle for Good,'" 39.

2. Deer, Zarestky, and Baumgartner, "'Learn How to Hustle for Good.'"

3. Steven D. Brown, Robert W. Lent, Kyle Telander, and Selena Tramayne, "Social Cognitive Career Theory, Conscientiousness, and Work Performance: A Meta-Analytic Path Analysis," *Journal of Vocational Behavior* 79, no. 1 (2011): 81–90, https://doi.org/10.1016/j.jvb.2010.11.009.

4. Deer, Zarestky, and Baumgartner, "'Learn How to Hustle for Good,'" 38.

5. Deer, Zarestky, and Baumgartner, "'Learn How to Hustle for Good,'" 39–40.

6. Deer, Zarestky, and Baumgartner, "'Learn How to Hustle for Good.'"

7. Deer, Zarestky, and Baumgartner, "'Learn How to Hustle for Good,'" 43.

8. Robert W. Lent and Frederick G. Lopez, "Cognitive Ties That Bind: A Tripartite View of Efficacy Beliefs in Growth-Promoting Relationships," *Journal of Social and Clinical Psychology* 21, no. 3 (2002): 256–86, https://doi.org/10.1521/jscp.21.3.256.22535.

9. Deer, Zarestky, and Baumgartner, "'Learn How to Hustle for Good,'" 43.

10. Deer, Zarestky, and Baumgartner, "'Learn How to Hustle for Good,'" 45.

11. Deer, Zarestky, and Baumgartner, "'Learn How to Hustle for Good,'" 42.

CHAPTER 5

1. Ron Claassen, Charlotte Tilkes, Phil Kader, and Douglas E. Noll, "Restorative Justice: A Framework for Fresno," *The Fresno Center for Restorative Justice Framework* (2000): 12, accessed from: https://www.iirp.edu/pdf/bc04_fresno.pdf.

2. Howard Zehr, *The Little Book of Restorative Justice* (Intercourse, PA: Good Books, 2002).

3. Gregory D. Paul, "Paradoxes of Restorative Justice in the Workplace," *Management Communication Quarterly* 31, no. 3 (2017): 380–408, https://doi.org/10.1177/0893318916681512.

4. Adapted from Zehr, *The Little Book of Restorative Justice*.

5. Lynn A. Stout, "The Toxic Side Effects of Shareholder Primacy," *University of Pennsylvania Law Review* 161, no. 7 (2013): 2003–23, https://www.jstor.org/stable/23527857.

6. "Statement on the Purpose of a Corporation," *Business Roundtable*, August 19, 2019, accessed from: https://opportunity.businessroundtable.org/ourcommitment/.

7. Sheri Bridges and J. Kline Harrison, "Employee Perceptions of Stakeholder Focus and Commitment to the Organization," *Journal of Managerial Issues* 15, no. 4 (2003): 498–509, https://www.jstor.org/stable/40604448.

8. Bridges and Harrison, "Employee Perceptions of Stakeholder Focus and Commitment to the Organization," 505–6.

9. Bridges and Harrison, "Employee Perceptions of Stakeholder Focus and Commitment to the Organization."

10. Barton Poulson, "A Third Voice: A Review of Empirical Research on the Psychological Outcomes of Restorative Justice," *Utah Law Review* 167 (2003): 167–204, accessed from: https://heinonline.org/HOL/Page?handle=hein.journals/utahlr2003&div=14&g_sent=1&casa_token=GPrVm-B1Wo0AAAAA:KQ1IsmOGkTbeTgyf2hxTdZjwECYNBplfMg2p8eH1cA22I5Vykdq6VgLhvXBYW-oBRzq7g80&collection=journals.

11. Petru Lucian Curşeu and Sandra G. L. Schruijer, "Does Conflict Shatter Trust or Does Trust Obliterate Conflict? Revisiting the Relationships between Team Diversity, Conflict, and Trust," *Group Dynamics: Theory, Research, and Practice* 14, no. 1 (2010): 66–79, https://doi.org/10.1037/a0017104.

12. "The Journey to Equity and Inclusion," *Society for Human Resource Management (SHRM)*, Summer (2020): 11, accessed from: https://shrmtogether.wpengine.com/wp-content/uploads/2020/08/20-1412_TFAW_Report_RND7_Pages.pdf.

13. Adrienne B. Hancock and Rubin A. Benjamin, "Influence of Communication Partner's Gender on Language." *Journal of Language and Social Psychology* 34, no. 1 (January 2015): 46–64, https://doi.org/10.1177/0261927X14533197.

14. Ruby K. Payne, *A Framework for Understanding Poverty: A Cognitive Approach*, 5th ed. (Highlands, TX: aha! Process, Inc., 2013).

CHAPTER 6

1. Deer, Zarestky, and Baumgartner, "'Learn How to Hustle for Good,'" 38.

2. Deer, Zarestky, and Baumgartner, "'Learn How to Hustle for Good.'"

3. Deer and Zarestky, "Balancing Profit and People," 728.

CHAPTER 7

1. Deer, Zarestky, and Baumgartner, "'Learn How to Hustle for Good.'"

2. Deer, Zarestky, and Baumgartner, "'Learn How to Hustle for Good.'"

3. Deer, Zarestky, and Baumgartner, "'Learn How to Hustle for Good,'" 41.

4. Shannon Deer, "'The Money . . . Was Far More of a Relapse for Me': A Qualitative Study of Women's Experiences Transitioning from the Sex Trade to Legal Employment," Paper presented at the 58th Annual Adult Education Research Conference Proceedings (Norman: University of Oklahoma, June 8–11, 2017): 4, accessed from: https://newprairiepress.org/aerc/2017/papers/24/.

5. Deer, "'The Money . . . Was Far More of a Relapse for Me,'" 4.

6. Deer, "'The Money . . . Was Far More of a Relapse for Me,'" 3.

7. Howard G. Birnbaum, Ronald C. Kessler, David Kelley, Rym Ben-Hamadi, Vijay N. Joish, and Paul E. Greenberg, "Employer Burden of Mild, Moderate, and Severe Major Depressive Disorder: Mental Health Services Utilization and Costs, and Work Performance," *Depression and Anxiety* 27, no. 1 (2010): 78–89, doi 10.1002/da.20580.

8. Deer, Zarestky, and Baumgartner, "'Learn How to Hustle for Good,'" 43.

9. Deer, Zarestky, and Baumgartner, "'Learn How to Hustle for Good,'" 41.

10. Deer, Zarestky, and Baumgartner, "'Learn How to Hustle for Good.'"

CHAPTER 8

1. United Nations, "The Sustainable Development Goals Report 2019," 2.

2. United Nations, "The Sustainable Development Goals Report 2019," 11.

3. United Nations, "The Sustainable Development Goals Report 2019," 15.

4. United Nations, "The Sustainable Development Goals Report 2019," 15.

5. Gordon Clark, Andreas Feiner, and Michael Viehs, "From the Stockholder to the Stakeholder—How Sustainability Can Drive Financial Outperformance," *Organizations and Markets: Formal and Informal Structures eJournal* (2015): 8, accessed from: https://papers.ssrn.com/sol3/papers.cfm?abstract_id=2508281.

6. PricewaterhouseCoopers, "Women in Work Index: Closing the Gender Pay Gap," March 2018, accessed from: https://www.pwc.com/hu/hu/csr/assets/women-in-work-index-2018.pdf.

7. McKinsey & Company, "Delivering through Diversity 2018 Report" (July 18, 2018): 1, accessed from: https://www.mckinsey.com/business-functions/organization/our-insights/delivering-through-diversity.

8. Bureau for Employers' Activities (ACT/EMP), "Women in Business Management: The Business Case for Change," International Labour Office (2019): iii, accessed from: https://www.ilo.org/wcmsp5/groups/public/---dgreports/---dcomm/---publ/documents/publication/wcms_700953.pdf.

9. SHRM and Charles Koch Institute, "Workers with Criminal Records: A Survey by the Society for Human Resource Management and the Charles Koch Institute," SHRM/CKI Survey Report (2018), accessed from: https://mk0qeluyepi9drvw7cng.kinstacdn.com/wp-content/uploads/2018/05/CKI-SHRM-Report.pdf.

10. Office of the Press Secretary, "FACT SHEET: White House Launches the Fair Chance Business Pledge," The White House: President Barak Obama, April 11, 2016, accessed from: https://obamawhitehouse.archives.gov/the-press-office/2016/04/11/fact-sheet-white-house-launches-fair-chance-business-pledge.

11. Rosalie Chan, "This call center company relies on a workforce of incarcerated women to help companies like Microsoft, SAP, and Dell power their sales and marketing," *Business Insider,* July 4, 2019, accessed from: https://www.businessinsider.com/televerde-incarcerated-women-perryville-arizona-indiana-2019-6.

12. Steve Corbett and Brian Fikkert, *When Helping Hurts: How to Alleviate Poverty Without Hurting the Poor . . . and Yourself* (Chicago, IL: Moody Publishers, 2014).

13. Howard Zehr, *Changing Lenses: Restorative Justice for Our Times*, New Edition, 25th Anniversary (Harrisonburg, VA: Herald Press, 2015).

14. Cheryl Miller, *Language of Shalom: 7 Keys to Practical Reconciliation* (Victoria, TX: Quantum Circles Press, 2012).

15. Bob Luddy, *Entrepreneurial Life: The Path From Startup to Market Leader* (Raleigh, NC: CaptiveAire, 2018).

APPENDIX

1. Judi Brownell, *Listening: Attitudes, Principles, and Skills*, 5th ed. (London: Pearson, 2012).

BIBLIOGRAPHY

Ambrose, Susan A., Michael W. Bridges, Michele DiPietro, Marsha C. Lovett, and Marie K. Norman. *How Learning Works: Seven Research-Based Principles for Smart Teaching.* San Francisco: Jossey-Bass, 2010.

Angelovksa, Ana. "Reshaping Reputation in the Workplace." *RepTrak*, July 22, 2019. Accessed from: https://www.reptrak.com/blog/reshaping -reputation-in-the-workplace/.

Auluck-Wilson, Clarice A. "When All Women Lift." *Signs*, Summer (1995): 1029–38. https://www.jstor.org/stable/3174894.

Balagot, James. "Inside Learning: How Yelp Created a Successful Learning Culture." *Continu*, September 1, 2017. Accessed from: https://blog .continu.co/yelp-successful-learning-culture/.

Birnbaum, Howard G., Ronald C. Kessler, David Kelley, Rym Ben-Hamadi, Vijay N. Joish, and Paul E. Greenberg. "Employer Burden of Mild, Moderate, and Severe Major Depressive Disorder: Mental Health Services Utilization and Costs, and Work Performance." *Depression and Anxiety* 27, no. 1 (2010): 78–89. doi 10.1002/da.20580.

Bloom, David E., Michael Kuhn, and Klaus Prettner. "Invest in Women and Prosper." *Finance and Development* 54, no. 3 (2017): 50–55. Accessed from: https://www.imf.org/external/pubs/ft/fandd/2017/09/bloom.htm.

Brandstätter, Hermann. "Personality Aspect of Entrepreneurship: A Look at Five Meta-Analyses." *Personality and Individual Differences* 51, no. 3 (2011): 222–30.

Bridges, Sheri, and J. Kline Harrison. "Employee Perceptions of Stakeholder Focus and Commitment to the Organization." *Journal of Managerial Issues* 15, no. 4 (2003): 498–509. https://www.jstor.org/stable/40604448.

Brooks, David. *The Second Mountain: The Quest for a Moral Life.* London, United Kingdom: Penguin, 2019.

Brown, Steven D., Robert W. Lent, Kyle Telander, and Selena Tramayne. "Social Cognitive Career Theory, Conscientiousness, and Work Performance: A Meta-Analytic Path Analysis." *Journal of Vocational Behavior* 79, no. 1 (2011): 81–90. https://doi.org/10.1016/j.jvb. 2010.11.009.

Brownell, Judi. *Listening: Attitudes, Principles, and Skills*, 5th ed. London: Pearson, 2012.

Bureau for Employers' Activities (ACT/EMP). "Women in Business Management: The Business Case for Change." *International Labour Office* (2019). Accessed from: https://www.ilo.org/wcmsp5/groups/public/---dgreports/---dcomm/---publ/documents/publication/wcms_700953.pdf.

Chan, Rosalie. "This call center company relies on a workforce of incarcerated women to help companies like Microsoft, SAP, and Dell power their sales and marketing." *Business Insider*, July 4, 2019. Accessed from: https://www.businessinsider.com/televerde-incarcerated-women-perryville-arizona-indiana-2019-6.

Claassen, Ron, Charlotte Tilkes, Phil Kader, and Douglas E. Noll. "Restorative Justice: A Framework for Fresno." *The Fresno Center for Restorative Justice Framework* (2000). Accessed from: https://www.iirp.edu/pdf/bc04_fresno.pdf.

Clark, Gordon, Andreas Feiner, and Michael Viehs. "From the Stockholder to the Stakeholder—How Sustainability Can Drive Financial Outperformance." *Organizations and Markets: Formal and Informal Structures eJournal* (2015). Accessed from: https://papers.ssrn.com/sol3/papers.cfm?abstract_id=2508281.

Cooperrider Center. "Who Uses Appreciative Inquiry?" Champlain College. Accessed October 25, 2020, from: https://www.champlain.edu/ai-home/what-is-appreciative-inquiry/who-uses-appreciative-inquiry.

———. "Why Appreciative Inquiry?" Champlain College. Accessed October 25, 2020, from: https://www.champlain.edu/ai-home/what-is-appreciative-inquiry/why-appreciative-inquiry.

Corbett, Steve, and Brian Fikkert, *When Helping Hurts: How to Alleviate Poverty Without Hurting the Poor . . . and Yourself.* Chicago, IL: Moody Publishers, 2014.

Curşeu, Petru Lucian, and Sandra G. L. Schruijer. "Does Conflict Shatter Trust or Does Trust Obliterate Conflict? Revisiting the Relationships between Team Diversity, Conflict, and Trust." *Group Dynamics: Theory, Research, and Practice* 14, no. 1 (2010): 66–79. https://doi.org/10.1037 /a0017104.

Deer, Shannon. "'The Money . . . Was Far More of a Relapse for Me': A Qualitative Study of Women's Experiences Transitioning from the Sex Trade to Legal Employment." Paper presented at the 58th Annual Adult Education Research Conference Proceedings. Norman: University of Oklahoma, June 8–11, 2017.

Deer, Shannon, and Lisa Baumgartner. "'I Can Relate': Survivor Leadership Supporting Women Transitioning out of the Sex Trade." *Adult Learning* 30, no. 4 (2019): 167–75. Accessed from: https://search.ebscohost.com /login.aspx?direct=true&db=eric&AN=EJ1231274&site=eds-live.

Deer, Shannon, and Jill Zarestky. "Balancing Profit and People: Corporate Social Responsibility in Business Education." *Journal of Management Education* 41, no. 5 (2017): 727–49. doi: 10.1177/1052562917719918.

Deer, Shannon, Jill Zarestky, and Lisa M. Baumgartner. "'Learn How to Hustle for Good': Women's Work Transitions out of the Sex Trade." *Human Resource Development* 31, no. 1 (2019): 31–48. doi: 10.1002/hrdq.21382.

Dewey, John. *Experience and Education.* New York: Collier Books, 1963.

Dove. "Welcome to the #GirlCollective." *Dove.com,* October 20, 2020. Accessed from: https://www.dove.com/us/en/stories/campaigns/girl-collective .html.

Ensher, Ellen A., Craig Thomas, and Susan E. Murphy. "Comparison of Transitional Step-Ahead, and Peer Mentoring on Protégés' Support, Satisfaction, and Perceptions of Career Success: A Social Exchange Perspective." *Journal of Business and Psychology* 15, no. 3 (2001): 419–38. doi: 10.1023/A:1007870600459.

Folbre, Nancy. *The Invisible Heart: Economics and Family Values.* New York: New Press, 2002.

Gates, Melinda. *The Moment of Lift: How Empowering Women Changes the World.* New York: Flatiron Books, 2019.

Google. "Google Environmental Report 2019." *Google.* Accessed October 20, 2020, from: https://sustainability.google/reports/environmental -report-2019/.

Hancock, Adrienne B., and Rubin A. Benjamin. "Influence of Communication Partner's Gender on Language." *Journal of Language and Social Psychology* 34, no. 1 (January 2015): 46–64. https://doi.org/10.1177 /0261927X14533197.

Hayton, James C., and Gabriella Cacciotti. "Is There an Entrepreneurial Culture? A Review of Empirical Research." *Entrepreneurship and Regional*

Development 25, nos. 9–10 (2013): 708–31. http://dx.doi.org/10.1080/089 85626.2013.862962.

Hiemstra, Djoerd, and Nico W. Van Yperen. "The Effects of Strength-Based Versus Deficit-Based Self-Regulated Learning Strategies on Students' Effort Intentions." *Motivation and Emotions* 39 (2015): 656–68. https://doi. org/10.1007/s11031-015-9488-8.

Hoddinott, John, and Lawrence Haddad. "Does Female Income Share Influence Household Expenditures? Evidence from Côte D'Ivoire." *Oxford Bulletin of Economics and Statistics* 57, no. 1 (1995): 77–96. doi: 10.1111 /j.1468-0084.1995.tb00028.x.

Hotaling, Norma, Autumn Burris, B. Julie Johnson, Yoshi M. Bird, and Kirsten A. Melbye. "Been There Done That: SAGE, A Peer Leadership Model among Prostitution Survivors." *Journal of Trauma Practice* 2 (2003): 255–65. doi:10.1300/J189v02n03_1.

Johnson & Johnson. 2019 Health for Humanity Report: Progress in Sustainability." Accessed October 20, 2020, from: https://healthforhumanity report.jnj.com/_document/2019-heath-for-humanity-report-johnson -johnson?id=00000172-a8f8-dff3-a9fa-acfda52c0000.

Kolb, David A. *Experiential Learning: Experience as the Source of Learning and Development.* Upper Saddle River, NJ: Pearson Education, 2015.

Lent, Robert W., and Frederick G. Lopez. "Cognitive Ties That Bind: A Tripartite View of Efficacy Beliefs in Growth-Promoting Relationships." *Journal of Social and Clinical Psychology* 21, no. 3(2002): 256–86. https:// doi.org/10.1521/jscp.21.3.256.22535.

Luddy, Bob. *Entrepreneurial Life: The Path From Startup to Market Leader.* Raleigh, NC: CaptiveAire, 2018.

Macy, Rebecca J., and Natalie Johns. "Aftercare Services for International Sex Trafficking Survivors: Informing U.S. Service and Program Development in an Emerging Practice Area." *Trauma, Violence, and Abuse* 12, no. 2 (2011): 87–98. doi:10.1177/1524838010390709.

Marques, Carla S., Sandra Valente, and Marisa Lages. "The Influence of Personal and Organisational Factors on Entrepreneurship Intention: An Application in the Health Care Sector." *Journal of Nursing Management* 26 (2018): 696–706.

McKinsey & Company. "Delivering through Diversity 2018 Report." July 18, 2018. Accessed from: https://www.mckinsey.com/business-functions /organization/our-insights/delivering-through-diversity.

Merriam, Sharan B., and Laura L. Bierema. *Adult Learning: Linking Theory and Practice.* San Francisco: Jossey-Bass, 2013.

Miller, Cheryl. *Language of Shalom: 7 Keys to Practical Reconciliation.* Victoria, TX: Quantum Circles Press, 2012.

O'Hagan, Mary. "Leadership for Empowerment and Equality: A Proposed Model for Mental Health User/Survivor Leadership." *The International Journal of Leadership in Public Services* 5, no. 4 (2009): 34–43. doi:10.5042/ijlps.2010.0110.

Office of the Press Secretary. "FACT SHEET: White House Launches the Fair Chance Business Pledge." The White House: President Barak Obama, April 11, 2016. Accessed from: https://obamawhitehouse.archives.gov /the-press-office/2016/04/11/fact-sheet-white-house-launches-fair-chance -business-pledge.

Paul, Gregory D. "Paradoxes of Restorative Justice in the Workplace." *Management Communication Quarterly* 31, no. 3 (2017): 380–408. https://doi .org/10.1177/0893318916681512.

Payne, Ruby K. *A Framework for Understanding Poverty: A Cognitive Approach*, 5th ed. Highlands, TX: aha! Process, Inc., 2013.

Pflum, Mary. "As Millennial Parents Demand Sustainable Toys, Lego Is Perfecting Plant-Based Bricks." *NBC News*, August 2, 2019. Accessed from: https://www.nbcnews.com/business/consumer/millennial-parents -demand-sustainable-toys-lego-perfecting-plant-based-bricks-n1038721.

Pinchot III, Gifford. "Four Definitions for the Intrapreneur." *The Pinchot Perspective*, October 30, 2017. Accessed from: https://www.pinchot .com/2017/10/four-definitions-for-the-intrapreneur.html.

Pinchot III, Gifford, and Elizabeth S. Pinchot. "Intra-Corporate Entrepreneurship," Fall 1978. Accessed from: https://drive.google.com/file/d /0B6GgwqtG-DKcSlpsbGRBZkZYSlk/view.

Pinho, Jose Carlos, and Elisabete Sampaio de Sá. "Personal Characteristics, Business Relationships and Entrepreneurial Performance: Some Empirical Evidence." *Journal of Small Business and Enterprise Development* 21, no. 2 (2014): 284–300.

Poulson, Barton. "A Third Voice: A Review of Empirical Research on the Psychological Outcomes of Restorative Justice." *Utah Law Review* 167, (2003): 167–204. Accessed from: https://heinonline.org/HOL/Page?handle=hein .journals/utahlr2003&div=14&g_sent=1&casa_token=GPrVm-B1Wo0AA AAA:KQ1IsmOGkTbeTgyf2hxTdZjwECYNBplfMg2p8eH1cA22I5Vykdq 6VgLhvXBYW-oBRzq7g80&collection=journals.

PricewaterhouseCoopers. "Women in Work Index: Closing the Gender Pay Gap." March 2018. Accessed from: https://www.pwc.com/hu/hu/csr/assets /women-in-work-index-2018.pdf.

Rauch, Andreas, and Michael Frese. "Let's Put the Person Back into Entrepreneurship Research: A Meta-Analysis on the Relationship between Business Owners' Personality Traits, Business Creation, and Success." *European Journal of Work and Organizational Psychology* 16, no. 4, (2007): 353–85.

Robinson, Peter B., David V. Stimpson, Jonathan C. Huefner, and H. Keith Hunt. "An Attitude Approach to the Prediction of Entrepreneurship." *Entrepreneurship: Theory and Practice* 15 (1991): 13–32. Accessed from: https://www.researchgate.net/profile/Jonathan_Huefner/publication/270820261_An_Attitude_Approach_to_the_Prediction_of_Entrepreneurship/links/55ef024008aedecb68fd8f02.pdf.

Shane, Scott, and Nicos Nicolaou. "Creative Personality, Opportunity Recognition and the Tendency to Start Businesses: A Study of Their Genetic Predispositions." *Journal of Business Ventures* 30, no. 3 (2015): 407–19.

SHRM, and Charles Koch Institute. "Workers with Criminal Records: A Survey by the Society for Human Resource Management and the Charles Koch Institute." SHRM/CKI Survey Report (2018). Accessed from: https://mk0qeluyepi9drvw7cng.kinstacdn.com/wp-content/uploads/2018/05/CKI-SHRM-Report.pdf.

Silberman, Mel. *The Handbook of Experiential Learning.* San Francisco: Pfeiffer, 2007.

"Statement on the Purpose of a Corporation." *Business Roundtable*, August 19, 2019. Accessed from: https://opportunity.businessroundtable.org/our commitment/.

Stout, Lynn A. "The Toxic Side Effects of Shareholder Primacy." *University of Pennsylvania Law Review* 161, no. 7 (2013): 2003–23. https://www.jstor.org/stable/23527857.

"The Journey to Equity and Inclusion." *Society for Human Resource Management (SHRM)*, Summer (2020): 11. Accessed from: https://shrmtogether.wpengine.com/wp-content/uploads/2020/08/20-1412_TFAW_Report_RND7_Pages.pdf.

United Nations. "The Sustainable Development Goals Report 2019." *UnitedNations.com.* Accessed from: https://unstats.un.org/sdgs/report/2019/.

Vygotsky, Lev S. *Mind in Society.* Cambridge, MA: Harvard University Press, 1978.

Wheatley, Margaret J. *Turning to One Another: Simple Conversations to Restore Hope to the Future.* San Francisco: Berrett-Koshler Publishers, Inc., 2002.

Zehr, Howard. *Changing Lenses: Restorative Justice for Our Times*, New Edition, 25th Anniversary. Harrisonburg, VA: Herald Press, 2015.

———. *The Little Book of Restorative Justice.* Intercourse, PA: Good Books, 2002.

INDEX

addiction, 5, 6, 9, 41, 65, 114, 142;
recovery, 7, 59, 158; relapse into,
153–54; skills learned, 26; as a
social identity, 145; substance
use, 8, 154; survivor leaders of,
36–39. *See also* relapse
American Airlines, 185
Apple, 42
asset-based approach, 40–41, 49,
169, 172; strength-based, 40–41
autonomy, 18, 24, 51–52, 62–63,
66–67

biases, overcoming, 6, 21, 162, 163,
175, 199
Brooks, David, 3

Child Protective Services (CPS), 31
CliftonStrengths, 42, 190
Coaches, 83–86, 167
The Coca-Cola Company, 42, 185
Corbett, Steve, 186

corporate social responsibility
(CSR), 1, 2, 138, 178; people,
planet, and profit, 1, 2, 176;
triple bottom line, 2, 176; people
and planet consciousness, 2. *See
also* sustainability
criminal record, 145–47, 185, 191

decent work, 71, 176–77; appealing
employment, 133; dignified
work, 157
deficit-based approach, 40–41, 44,
49; needs-based, 40; O'Hagan,
40
Department of Corrections (DOC),
97, 126
discovery-based learning, 15, 19, 20,
24–25, 51, 52, 169, 179, 181. *See
also* experiential learning
diversity, 2, 85, 163–64; diverse
ideas, 73; diverse perspectives,
132, 139, 164, 172, 191;

ABOUT THE AUTHORS

Shannon Deer, PhD, CPA, is the interim associate dean for undergraduate programs and a clinical assistant professor for Mays Business School at Texas A&M University. She is an award-winning professor who prepares experienced professionals in Texas A&M's MBA programs for successful careers in business. She also conducts executive development training for leading companies. Deer's research, included in this book, has been published in leading, peer-reviewed journals. Her research focuses on women's transitional experience after exiting the sex trade or sex-trafficking situations. She specifically focuses on the impact (positive and negative) businesses have on survivors in their work transition. Deer researched many of the principles in this book. She lives in College Station, Texas, with her husband, dogs, sometimes chickens, and the screened in porch where she writes.

Cheryl Miller owns Quantum Circles Consulting and Training. She provides training on topics that increase opportunities for transformation in three areas: economic development for the marginalized, effective communication focusing on the facilitation of conflict, and restorative justice. Miller has been a volunteer mediator for sixteen

years and has more than a thousand hours of experience of mediation with victims of violent crimes and their offenders. She was
the executive director of a housing program in Victoria, Texas, for
eighteen years. The typical population of the home incudes women
with long-term substance abuse, ex-offenders, and women in the sex
industry. Miller could relate to some of the women's experience after
being a single mom to premature twins and on welfare. She used the
principles in this book to create an empowerment support model for
women at the home. Cheryl lives in Victoria, Texas, with her husband
and chickens, and travels as often as possible to see her grown children and grandchildren.